POETICS:
An Illustrated Guide

Steven Reeder, Oksun Kang
Illustrator, Hyosun An

Shinasa

Table of Contents

OUT OF OLD MYTHOLOGIES:

A Prologue

From the beginning of civilization, people have tried to give expression to the world they experience. This is often done with some type of rhythm called poetry. It is the most significant expression of thoughts brought forth into the spoken word. What makes poetry great is that it expresses ideas and feelings in ways that others can relate to. It gives thoughts a type of form. The poet must choose the right words to make these images concrete. John Milton found poetry to be "simple, sensuous, and impassioned."

The first function of poetry is to please the senses. Poets explain sights, sound, and colors in ways that produce these images in the reader's minds. This is often accomplished in a musical form. Poetry is found in every aspect of creative expression: in songs, dramas, stories, myths, even in modern popular music. No one can resist its attraction. A life without poetry of any kind is life without enjoyment.

The purpose of this book is to bring the enjoyment of reading poetry to second language learners. To assist the beginner, we, the editors, have divided this book of poetry into two sections. The first is themes. There are various themes that can be found in poetry, but the four that we found to be the most inspiring are themes of love, personal identity, solitude, and freedom. The second section is elements of poetry. Again, there are so many elements to choose from that we had to limit ourselves to just five: diction, syntax, irony and paradox, figures of speech, and the sound of poetry.

Within each unit, we have attempted to make the poems as accessible as possible. First, we start off with a simple explanation of what each unit means to each section. Sample poems are provided that best highlight the idea of the unit. For any words that are archaic or may be difficult to define, even with a dictionary, we have provided footnotes. After every poem, an explanation of the poem is given, and for the more difficult poems, a summary of meaning. When necessary, historical background that had a major influence on the time is given. This is necessary since writers often expected the reader to understand what was occurring when the piece was written. Without knowledge of this, the poems tend to be archaic and stuck in the past. Also, major periods like the Romantic Period that were influenced by the historical background are introduced. These periods drew intellectuals and writers together and often led to movements like Imagism or the Oxford Movement. Finally, a biography of a major poet is offered to give more insight into his or her life, the poetry written, and the time he or she was born in.

A new addition to this book is the art. We wanted to add a visual aspect to an art form that can be difficult for beginners. This adds a whole new dimension to the understanding of a poem that may assist the beginner with a fresher understanding. Finally, key literary words are highlighted throughout the text and can be found in the glossary. Most of the more difficult words are defined within the text itself, but when encountered again, the student may easily find them in the back.

It is our hope that this text will be interesting and informative to any student or teacher of poetry at the introductory level. There is quite a lot of information packed into this book, but it is our goal that this short guide will lead the reader to a greater desire to read more poetry and enjoy it as much as we do.

Steven Reeder
Kyungsung University

PART I

THEMES

THEME ONE: LOVE

Love as a word is difficult enough to comprehend let alone explain. It took the ancient Greek philosopher Plato seven lengthy dialogues to come to an understanding of what love is. Our task in this chapter is a little less daunting and far simpler. We are going to tackle the idea of love with eleven simple poems by some of England's most respected poets.

Love is often ambiguous. And like love, a poet's tone is just as unclear. But what is clear are the intentions of all the male poets featured. We will look at the ideas expressed in Plato's *Symposium* (385 BCE) through just two characters: Pausanias and Aristophanes.

First, Pausanias expresses the idea of both spiritual and vulgar love. Spiritual love is what we now call Platonic love, a more intellectual relationship between two people, and is more concerned with loving the soul of a person. On the other hand, vulgar love is the base sexual desire and is often expressed in male poetics as *carpe diem*, Latin for "seize the day!" In Elizabethan times, *carpe diem* poetry was used to remind the readers to live life to the fullest and not to waste love with shyness since time and youth are temporary. The phrase is a classical idea that dates to Roman times when the poet Horace (circa 65 B.C.-8 B.C.) wrote, "Seize the day, trust tomorrow as little as possible."

A fine example of a *carpe diem* poem is Ben Jonson's "Song: To Celia," a more traditional variant of seizing the day.

SONG: TO CELIA

Ben Jonson (1572-1637)

Drink to me only with thine[1] eyes,
And I will pledge with mine;
Or leave a kiss but in the cup,
And I'll not look for wine.
The thirst that from the soul doth[2] rise,
Doth ask a drink divine:
But might I of Jove's[3] nectar sup[4],
I would not change for thine[5].

I sent thee[6] late a rosy wreath,
Not so much honoring thee,
As giving it a hope, that there
It could not withered be.
But thou thereon did'st[7] only breathe,
And sent'st it back to me;
Since when it grows and smells, I swear,
Not of itself, but thee.

1 thine: (prn) old form of yours

2 doth: (v) old form of does

3 Jove: (n) Roman for Zeus

4 sup: (v) to eat supper

5 thine: (prn) old form of yours

6 thee: (prn) old form of you

7 'st: old form to mark 2nd person singular

Here Jonson uses memorable **metaphor**s to sing praises of a woman's beauty. He was rephrasing famous lines from the *Epistles of Philostratus* written in the third century A.D. Compare Philostratus' *Letter XXIV*, "Drink to me with thine eyes only. Or, if thou wilt, putting the cup to thy lips, fill it with kisses, and so bestow it upon me," with the opening lines in Jonson's poem: "Drink to me, only with thine eyes / And I will pledge with mine; / Or leave a kiss but in the cup." There is a romantic quality to the verse and rhyme scheme that would make any woman swoon, which is exactly the role of *carpe diem* poetry.

Modern critics would criticize this style of poetry as sentimental and singular in goal—to have a woman fall for the man—yet Jonson has avoided that with the easy flowing use of both **assonance** (Or leave a **k**iss but in the **c**up; **D**oth ask a **d**rink **d**ivine) and **hyperbole** (saying her kiss is greater than the nectar of the gods). Every word and stress flows beautifully into an unsung song that sends hearts aflutter. Notice, as well, that Jonson seems just as interested in the woman's soul as he is with her body.

Another fine example of a *carpe diem* poem is Andrew Marvell's "To His Coy Mistress".

TO HIS COY[8] MISTRESS

Andrew Marvell (1621-1678)

Had we but world enough, and time,
This coyness, lady, were no crime.
We would sit down, and think which way
To walk, and pass our long love's day.
Thou by the Indian Ganges'[9] side
Shouldst rubies find; I by the tide

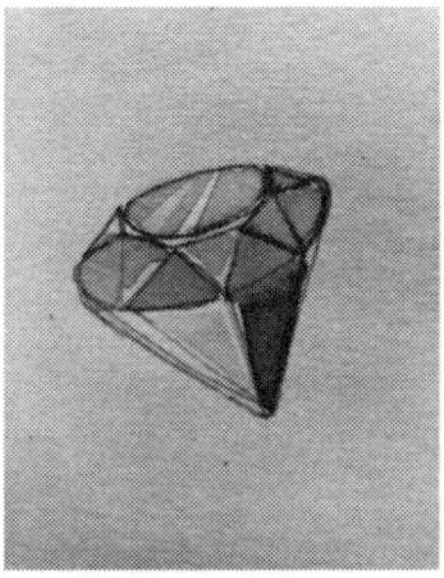

Of Humber[10] would complain.[11] I would
Love you ten years before the Flood,[12]
And you should, if you please, refuse
Till the conversion of the Jews.[13]
My vegetable love should grow
Vaster than empires, and more slow;
An hundred years should go to praise

8 coy: (adj) shy or modest

9 Ganges: a sacred river in India; considered sacred

10 Humber: a small muddy river in Trent, England

11 complain: (v) poetic for 'moaning plaintive poems of love"

12 the Flood: the great Biblical Flood in the time of Noah

13 conversion of the Jews: a popular Christian motif having the Jews convert just before the Last Judgment of God

Thine eyes, and on thy forehead gaze;
Two hundred to adore each breast,
But thirty thousand to the rest;
An age at least to every part,
And the last age should show your heart.
For, lady, you deserve this state,
Nor would I love at lower rate.
But at my back I always hear
Time's wingéd chariot hurrying near;
And yonder[14] all before us lie
Deserts of vast eternity.

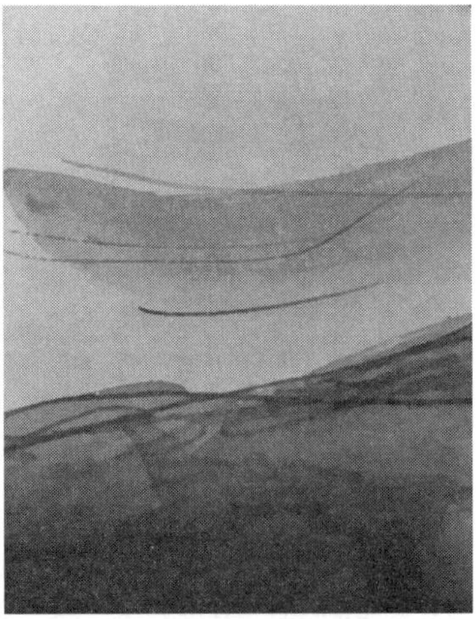

Thy beauty shall no more be found,
Nor, in thy marble vault shall sound
My echoing song; then worms shall try
That long-preserved virginity,
And your quaint honor turn to dust,
And into ashes all my lust:

14 yonder: (adj) over there

The grave's a fine and private place,
But none, I think, do there embrace.
Now therefore, while the youthful hue[15]
Sits on thy skin like morning dew,

And while thy willing soul transpires[16]
At every pore with instant fires,[17]
Now let us sport us while we may,
And now, like amorous[18] birds of prey,
Rather at once our time devour
Than languish in his slow-chapped[19] power.
Let us roll all our strength and all
Our sweetness up into one ball,
And tear our pleasures with rough strife[20]
Thorough[21] the iron gates of life.
Thus, though we cannot make our sun
Stand still, yet we will make him run.

15 hue: (n) color

16 transpire: (v) emit

17 instant fires: immediate passion

18 amorous: (adj) showing love

19 slow-chapped: also meaning 'slow-jawed'; a metaphor for time slowly eating the world and people

20 strife: (n) struggle

21 thorough: (adj) old form meaning 'through'

The poem is opposite in nature to Jonson's previous one. Where Jonson uses common English ideas that marry symbol and image, Marvell takes a step further by writing **paradox** with grand, **epic** ideas that span the globe.

He invokes images of his humble hometown river of Humber with the magical river Ganges in India (paradoxical). He speaks of loving her from the time of Noah—the mythological time that humanity started over—to the conversion of the Jews, which is supposed to take place at the end of the world according to the "Book of Revelations" in the Bible. A comparison of images that Jonson uses (cups, kisses, souls, gods, nectar, wreaths) with Marvell' s (the Flood, conversion of the Jews, vegetable love, forehead, deserts, ashes, graves, pores, birds of prey, iron gates of life) shows that "To His Coy Mistress" uses imagery not normally related to love poetry (see also John Donne's "The Flea").

Marvell does exceed Jonson with the **hyperbole**, and his overuse of it only affirms the *carpe diem* idea that there is not a better time than now for love making. Remember that it is not the fact that the narrator isn't getting any love from his mistress, it is because he isn't getting enough. There lies the desperation and turns the poem from crass love making into romanticism.

Metaphysical Poets

Metaphysical was a term applied to poetry that showed witty tricks in style. It was a term not used by any of the poets in their time but was later used to refer to a collective style connecting all their poetry. It was first used by John Dryden (1631-1700) to describe John Donne's writing, and then Samuel Jonson (1709-84) referred to that period in a negative sense using that term.

Metaphysical was how poetry was written and not what was written about. In other words, metaphysical poetry was not philosophical in nature. Instead of expressing an emotion in classical language, the poet chose to express and define his emotion, often with more "modern" terminology. By the time of John Donne (1571-1631), the Petrarchan sonnet form had been established and overused. Even Shakespeare tried to challenge and reverse the convention of addressing the mistress. John Donne and the other metaphysical poets found that there was not much more to say about love in the classical sense, but there still was a lot more to say about love.

No one poet can be considered as being part of a metaphysical school since all were so different from the other. They did share some similar characteristics that can be noted as the metaphysical style. They all commonly used

conceit, **paradox**, **puns**, and **word play** in their poems. They used **imagery** from seemingly unrelated sources of knowledge. Theology and science, geography and philosophy are often mixed in witty ways. Most of these images were shocking or scandalous. They tried to move poetry away from the flowery classical style to a more everyday type of speech.

Critics have noted that metaphysical poets wrote moments of powerful experiences but rarely created it. Metaphysical poets used their poems to argue, coax, or describe what was happening, so there was a lot of emotion expressed without the pay off. More than the love making itself, they needed to recognize experience in an academic, rational sense. Thus, they chose love, nature, and religion as common subjects because these offered a powerful spiritual moment. Then the poets took apart, explored, and pushed their point of view onto the reader about the experience.

Compare Shakespeare's classical style with Donne's metaphysical style:

> Shall I compare thee to a summer's day?
> Thou are more lovely and more temperate.

Most women would probably feel very pleased with being compared to a summer's day, such a simple comparison. Now look at Donne:

> Mark but this flea, and mark in this,
> How little that which thou deniest me is.

Donne basically says that her denying his love making is as insignificant as the flea! Shock was the impression these poets wished to give. The metaphysical poets were passionate but questioned and justified their emotions too much. Since their poems were not published or given to the public, the metaphysical poets wrote highly personal ones. If the poems were circulated, they were amongst the courts for only a few to see. The personal nature of these poems allowed the poets to be shocking in ways that most other poets dared not be.

One popular characteristic of the time is called the **metaphysical conceit**, a paradoxical, complex, and often shocking comparison of one idea with another. For example, Donne used the conceit of a flea biting his lover as a symbol of their blood mixing.

THE FLEA

John Donne (1572-1631)

Mark but this flea, and mark in this,
How little that which thou deny'st me is;
It sucked me first, and now sucks thee,
And in this flea our two bloods mingled be;
Thou know'st that this cannot be said
A sin, nor shame, nor loss of maidenhead,
Yet this enjoys before it woo,
And pampered swells with one blood made of two,
And this, alas, is more than we would do.

Oh stay, three lives in one flea spare,
Where we almost, yea more then married are,
This flea is you and I, and this
Our marriage bed, and marriage temple is;
Though parents grudge, and you, we're met,
And cloistered in these living walls of jet.
Though use[22] make you apt to kill me,
Let not to that, self-murder added be,
And sacrilege, three sins in killing three.

Cruel and sudden, hast thou since
Purpled thy nail, in blood of innocence?
Wherein could this flea guilty be,
Except in that drop it sucked from thee?
Yet thou triumph'st, and say'st that thou
Find'st not thyself, nor me, the weaker now;
　　'Tis true; then learn how false, fears be;
　　Just so much honor, when thou yield'st to me,
　　Will waste, as this flea's death took life from thee.

22 custom

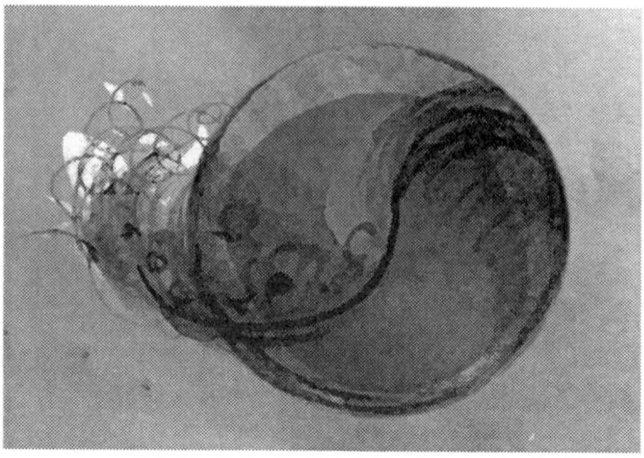

"The Flea" inverts the idea of romanticism by going from romantic to crass. Donne also shows us Aristophanes's argument as to why we need love as also found in Plato's *Symposium.* Aristophanes illustrates our pursuit of the opposite sex through a mythic tale of a time when people were round and composed of both male and female parts. When they challenged Zeus's authority, he cut them in half with a lightning bolt, causing both halves to search endlessly for the other. This explains why we feel empty without our better half.

In "The Flea," the narrator, lying in bed with his love, has picked up a flea that has bitten him and then jumped over to her. Probably landing on her breast, it has just bitten her. A common theory in Donne's day was that sexual relation was a mixing of a man's and woman' s blood; therefore, he compares their love making to the mixing of their blood in the flea. If such a mixing of blood with a flea does not bother the woman, then how could their own love making? And since they have become "one flesh" in the flea, they are, practically speaking, married; thus, they have all the legal and moral right to make love.

The maiden's prompt reply is to squish the flea with her finger. The narrator claims this is like murder since both their blood resides in the flea. Because killing the flea and committing sacrilege was so simple, then it should be just as easy to give in to the man' s demands for love making. Here, *carpe diem* is at its most urgent with the full blessing of God, as is seen in all the religious imagery used, for to deny the narrator his need for love making is to commit heresy; she is denying the very primal urge to be whole again.

The Metaphysical poets also used simple verse forms to express **paradox**, an absurd or contradictory statement that can be found truthful upon further thought. They joined together ideas from widely different areas of experience. The poet would explain mysteries of faith into language borrowed from science, medicine, mechanics, or war. For example, Andrew Marvell writes in "To His Coy Mistress":

> Thy beauty shall no more be found,
> Nor, in thy marble vault, shall sound
> My echoing song; then worms shall try
> That long-preserved virginity.

The narrator tells his lover that if she keeps her church sanctioned virginity until her death, it will be the worms that will steal it from her (by crawling through her body). And how much better is it for her if he took her virginity and not the worms! It may seem shocking, and might not make sense (a paradox), but there is a logic to what he writes. In life or death, we will sin. It is better to sin in life, so we can repent later; there is no repentance in death!

In love poetry, the metaphysical poets deal with central paradoxes of religious doctrine. Some examples of such paradoxes are as follows: The rebellious sinner desires God's love, as in George Herbert's "The Collar," (1633):

But as I raved and grew more fierce and wild
At every word,
Me thoughts I heard one calling, Child!
And I replied, My Lord.

Also, we all must die, but there is a life after death, such as in Donne's "Holy Sonnet X" (1633):

One short sleep past, we wake eternally,
And death shall be no more; Death, thou shalt die!

A Brief Introduction to John Donne

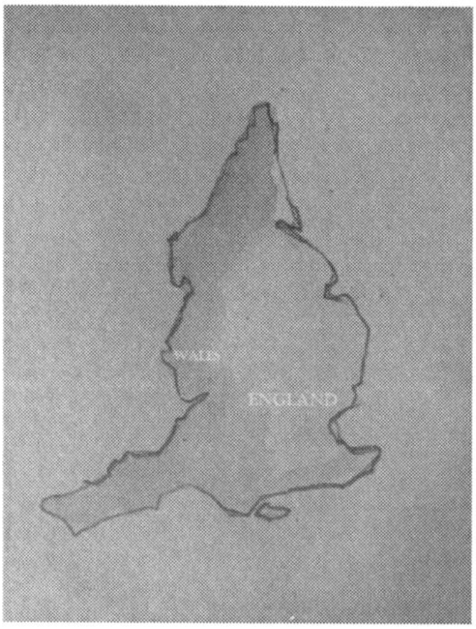

John Donne is considered the greatest of all the metaphysical poets. There was effort on his part, along with the other lesser poets that followed in his footsteps, to move away from the style of the times. He did not want to write images of nature or to rely on classical literature. Instead of using images and ideas of the past, he and other metaphysical poets referenced images found in the scientific discoveries of their time. Thus, religious and moral questions could be studied with one eye on beauty and the other on scientific principles. The argument of science and religion was very much alive in Donne's day. The great astronomers Copernicus and Galileo were as much Donne's contemporaries and the minds of his days as Einstein was in ours. Plus, Donne never took sides. He simply used the ideas of his day to better understand the inner turmoil of our souls.

Donne was educated as a Roman Catholic, but in 1615, he became an Anglican Priest (of the Church of England) on the insistence of King James I. His fame at this time came from his very popular sermons. His use of **conceits** can be found in the paradox of the magnificent scientific discoveries made in his time. Though great discoveries were occurring regularly, everything and everyone were still small and insignificant compared to the glory of God.

Donne's religious poetry uses conceit, for at times it reads like love poetry. Donne sometimes talks to God as if there were a conversation between two lovers.

John Donne first wrote only for a select few readers and not for mass publication. He was the first to start using the metaphysical conceits. Perhaps his easiest to understand, and most popular, is "A Valediction: Forbidding Mourning" (1611).

A VALEDICTION: FORBIDDING MOURNING

John Donne

As virtuous men pass mildly away,
And whisper to their souls to go,
Whilst some of their sad friends do say,
"Now his breath goes,[23]" and some say, "No."

So let us melt, and make no noise,
No tear-floods, nor sigh-tempests move;
'Twere profanation[24] of our joys
To tell the laity[25] our love.

Moving of th' earth brings harms and fears;
Men reckon what it did, and meant;

23 Now his breath goes: dies

24 profanation: (n) defilement

25 laity: (n) a congregation of worshippers in a church

But trepidation of the spheres,[26]
Though greater far, is innocent.
Dull sublunary[27] lovers' love
—Whose soul is sense—cannot admit
Of absence, 'cause it doth remove
The thing which elemented[28] it.

But we by a love so much refined,
That ourselves know not what it is,
Inter-assurèd[29] of the mind,
Care less, eyes, lips and hands to miss.

Our two souls therefore, which are one,
Though I must go, endure not yet
A breach, but an expansion,
Like gold to aery[30] thinness beat.

If they be two, they are two so
As stiff twin compasses[31] are two;
Thy soul, the fixed foot,[32] makes no show
To move, but doth, if th' other do.

And though it in the centre sit,

---

26 trepidation of the spheres: a reference to the then misunderstanding where astronomers thought planets moved in perfect circular orbits. When this did not happen, it was called the shaking of the spheres because of the earth wobbling on its axis.

27 sublunary: (adj) beneath the moon; sublunary lovers are earth bound and subject to the change experienced on earth

28 elemented: (v) old form meaning 'created'

29 interassured: (v) to know for sure

30 aery: (adj) composed of air

31 compass: (n) a drawing instrument that is used to draw a perfect circle

32 fixed foot: the pointed end of the compass that serves as the anchor

Yet, when the other[33] far doth roam,
It leans, and hearkens after it,
And grows erect, as that comes home.
Such wilt thou be to me, who must,
Like th' other foot, obliquely run;
Thy firmness makes my circle just,
And makes me end where I begun.

33 the other: the other end of the compass that moves around the center

Donne wrote this poem to his wife when he travelled to Europe and felt that something bad would happen to her. Something bad did happen. She gave birth to a stillborn child. In this poem, Donne uses the concept of conceit in a rather interesting way. Instead of addressing vulgar love as he does in "The Flea," Donne addresses a spiritual love. Probably since it was a poem written for his wife upon his departure, he tries to connect with her in a spiritual way. The conceit is comparing their love to gold and the compass—as opposed to flowers and sunsets.

Though I go, endure not yet
A breach, but an expansion,
Like gold to aery thinness beat.

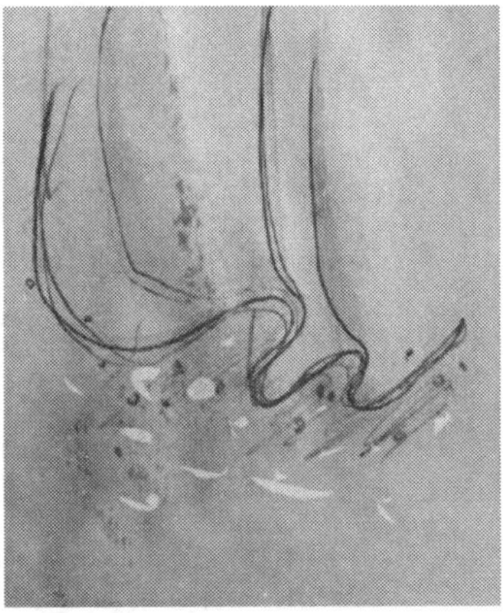

Upon first reading, it might seem cold and uncaring to compare their love in such a way. However, there is a method to this so-called madness. Though Donne must leave his wife behind on his trip, their souls are still one. They are not truly departing. Just as gold can be stretched "to aery thinness," their shared souls being so much purer, can stretch even more and fill the long distances between them.

If they be two, they are two so
As stiff twin compasses are two;
Thy soul, the fixed foot, makes no show
To move, but doth, if th' other do.

And if that is rejected and their souls are indeed separate, then they are like the feet of a compass.

And though in center sit,
Yet, when the far doth roam,
It leans, and hearkens after it,
And erect, as that comes home.

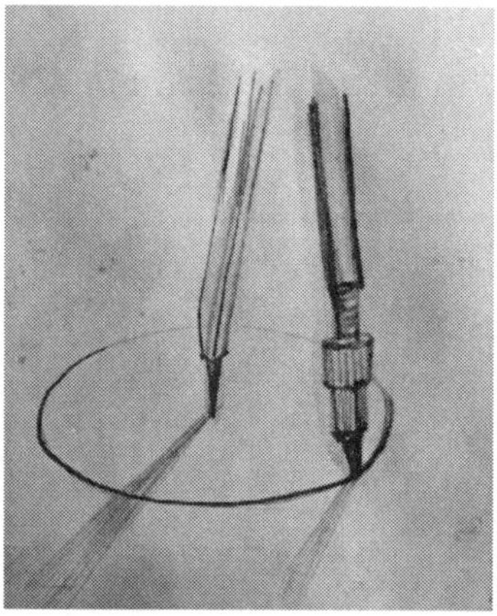

She is fixed at the center, and he moves around it in a perfect circle. The firmness of the center makes the outer foot move in perfect harmony.

Such wilt thou be to me, who must,
Like th' other foot, obliquely run;
Thy firmness makes my circle just,
And makes me end where I begun.

Donne had sacrificed his entire career for his wife, Anne More. While working as chief secretary for Lord Egerton, Donne fell in love with Egerton's niece and secretly married her. Both Egerton and Ann's father were upset over their marriage, and they imprisoned Donne until it was proven that their marriage was legitimate. After his release, he lost his job and position, being forced to retire at the age of 29. He lived the rest of his life in poverty. He relied on the patronage system of the court to make money with his poems. Finally, at the age of 49, Donne was given a high paying position as Dean of St. Paul's in the Church of England, a position he held for 10 years until his death in 1631.

A Brief Introduction to John Milton

(1608-1674)

Milton wrote during the time of the Metaphysical Poets, but he was in a class all his own. After Shakespeare, Milton is considered the next major poet. Milton saw himself as England's spokesperson and prophetic-bard. He attended Cambridge University and wrote several of his famous poems there, such as "L'Allegro" and "Il Penseroso," though they would not be published till his late 30's. Upon graduation, he continued his personal studies and learned six languages. Through his intensive studies, he became the most learned poet in the English language. He travelled through Italy and France to continue his education. While in Italy, he discovered the beauty of Roman Catholicism but saw it as too excessive.

Upon his return to England, Milton supported the Puritan cause and got involved in parliamentary politics. Milton, like other Puritans, was in direct opposition to the bishops, the remnants of Catholicism, and he wished to see them pushed out of the church completely. The Puritans also wanted to see the Church of England purged of all remaining Catholic ideas and corruption. Milton was especially not pleased with the Church of England and was against the policies of the Archbishop Laud. When the English Civil War broke out, Milton was separated from his wife for years, and he wished for a divorce. His anti-authority writings got him in trouble, and many of his works were censored. This led him to write "Areopagitica" (1644), his now famous anti-censorship poem.

During the English Civil War, Milton had supported Cromwell and the Commonwealth. He was even appointed a government position. He used his writing skills to defend Republican ideals. Ironically, his position led him to be a censor. He was also a strong supporter of the beheading of King Charles I. These views would get him into trouble later in his life and would even make him unpopular long after his death.

By the time of Cromwell's death and the collapse of the Republic, Milton had become impoverished and started work on his magnum opus, *Paradise Lost* from 1658 to 1664. Going blind, he had to dictate the **epic** poem for his aids, mostly his three daughters, to write down. It was unique for its time, for it was written in **free verse**, a poetic form that does not rhyme. With the restoration of the monarchy in 1660, Milton still strongly supported a Republic. A warrant for his arrest was issued, and he had to go into hiding. By this time, Milton had become completely blind. His past affiliation with Cromwell led him to a prison cell for a short time. Only through the persuasion of Andrew Marvell was he allowed to return to his home.

PARADISE LOST

WHEN I CONSIDER HOW MY LIGHT IS SPENT

John Milton

When I consider how my light is spent,
Ere[34] half my days in this dark world and wide,
And that one talent which is death to hide
Lodged with me useless, though my soul more bent
To serve therewith my Maker,[35] and present
My true account, lest He returning chide;[36]
"Doth God exact day-labor, light denied?"

I fondly ask. But Patience, to prevent
That murmur, soon replies, "God doth not need
Either man's work or His own gifts. Who best

34 Ere: (conj) before

35 Maker: God

36 chide: (v) scold

Bear His mild yoke,[37] they serve Him best. His state
Is kingly: thousands at His bidding speed,
And post o'er land and ocean without rest;
They also serve who only stand and wait."

37 yoke: (n) a wooden frame joining two animals; a symbol of subjection

This sonnet shows how Milton struggled with his blindness. The theme of a sonnet is usually set up in the **octave**, with the **sestet** introducing the **volta**, an unexpected or surprising thematic twist, in line nine. Here, in the octave, the speaker contemplates how God will judge him. The third line mentions "that one talent which is death to hide," referencing the parable Jesus relates in the Bible about the talent in Matthew 25:14-30. A talent is a coin that a servant is given by his master to make more money with. One servant buries it; two others set out to invest the talent. The first loses all his money while the second makes more money with the talent. The servant who hid the talent is the one in trouble by the master. The same can be said of those who hide their own talents or abilities.

The speaker in Milton's poem then asks a rhetorical question about God being a task master who demands work in exchange for "light" or spiritual illumination. The volta is God's unexpected response that follows through the rest of the sestet. God reminds the speaker that He does not require work or need it but blesses those who are willing to serve Him with an open heart. It is not what one does; but how one does it. Even as he was losing his sight, Milton did not wallow in misery or self-pity. He made sure he worked hard for what he believed in, no matter who was ruling the country, even if it meant dying for those beliefs.

The Romantic Period (1785-1830)

The fine line that separated the Romantic Period from the Neo-classical period before and the Victorian Age after was the publication of William Wordsworth's groundbreaking *Lyrical Ballads* in 1798 and the death of Sir Walter Scott in 1832. The writers of this time did not think of themselves as "Romantic writers." It was a term made up by historians fifty years later. The Big Six writers—Wordsworth, Coleridge, Byron, Percy Shelley, and Keats—were singled out by historians, who added William Blake later.

Women writers were very active in this time as well, but they were excluded from the canon until the late 20th century. Even among the Big Six, there was no consolidation of style or philosophy. William Wordsworth and Samuel Taylor Coleridge, who were in daily contact, did not hold the same ideas. Interestingly, when Wordsworth and Coleridge published their *Lyrical Ballads* (1798), Wordsworth was an unknown, and Coleridge was largely hated. The women writers, such as Anna Barbauld, Charlotte Smith, and Mary Robinson were the best-known poets of the time. Mary Robinson was the editor of the *Morning Post*, whom both men respected as they were struggling with their own craft.

There were "schools" that poets and their followers had been characterized as following, such as the Lake School of Wordsworth and Coleridge, and the Satanic School of Byron and Percy Shelley. There was, however, a certain spirit of the age that all the poets felt they were participating in—a kind of intellectual and creative environment. If anything, the Romantic Period was a reaction against the neoclassical literature that came before, and the rigid orthodoxy of style and thought. The orderly and polished neoclassical poetry was void of feeling for nature, and the heroic couplet was the popular form.

No longer did the poet have to be a born genius, where strict rules of classical poetry had to be studied and obeyed. A poet who was conscious of the inner emotion could create art that was open and free, honest and liberating.

The ideas of classical poetry, where the reader was forced to observe what the poet saw was now replaced by nature poetry with human characteristics. Like the revolutions in America and later in France, the Romantic Period was a liberal movement, a freeing of the artists from any restraints of the past imposed by religious or political rules. Thus, the formation of this period was highly influenced by the revolutions that surrounded it.

Many Romantic poets looked back upon Milton as a great poet-prophet. Like Milton, they would speak of moral truths to guide their generation through the chaos of their times. Thus, most romantic poets used the French Revolution as an example of hope for liberation from their own worries and troubles.

For the most part, the revolutionary spirit sparked by the American and the much more influential French Revolution brought a new hope of change and eventual peace to uneasy times. There was hope that old customs and thinking would disappear for fresher ideas. For the first time, the common people thought change could occur and make their lives better.

In an era of scientific, political, and religious propaganda, the Romantic Period was an island of calm, calling for a return to the imagination over the cold harsh laws of reason. Facts and realism were for the sciences, imagination was for the arts, which also included the religious and political arena. The world needed imagination to cure it of its ills, not reason. The sciences provided cold, unfeeling progress; the arts, therefore, should provide imagination and spirit, the balance. However, the French Revolution failed, and Napoleon became emperor, threatening all of Europe and Britain especially. Thus, Romantic poets who verbally supported the Revolution eventually publicly dismissed it with great disappointment.

A Brief Introduction to William Wordsworth (1770-1850)

As the head of the Romantic Movement in England and as one of the greatest poets in the English language, William Wordsworth championed the language of the ordinary people to describe commonplace ideas and things. Born in the countryside of the English Lake District, Wordsworth learned firsthand about the beauties of nature. At a young age, he lost both his parents and received a large inheritance that allowed him to travel through Europe and comfortably live the quiet life of a poet.

He was educated with his friend Samuel Taylor Coleridge but found that actual experience would benefit him better than book learning, so he traveled through France and the Alps on foot. He wrote of these experiences in *The Prelude*, first published in 1799, but reprinted throughout his life. He returned to England to finish his education and then returned to France in 1791 to learn the language fluently. It was during this time that he witnessed the first part of the French Revolution and became an outspoken supporter of it. He returned to England a year later.

When England declared war on Revolutionary France in 1793, Wordsworth suffered mental anguish between the two countries he had called home. His outspoken sympathies for the French made it so he could not hold any political office. Not until the Revolution's failure did Wordsworth become disillusioned with the cause, and he fell into depression. In 1797, Wordsworth retired into the country with his sister Dorothy, who would act as his secretary, and wrote poetry. Coleridge lived in another cottage close by, and the two of them conversed daily about the art of poetry. They co-wrote *Lyrical Ballads* (1798), the ultimate poetic manifesto followed by all Romantic poets. "She Dwelt among Untrodden Ways" first appeared in *Lyrical Ballads*.

SHE DWELT AMONG UNTRODDEN WAYS

William Wordsworth

She dwelt among the untrodden ways
Beside the springs of Dove,
Maid whom there were none to praise
And very few to love:

A violet by a mossy tone
Half hidden from the eye!
Fair as a star, when only one
Is shining in the sky.

She lived unknown, and few could know
When Lucy ceased to be;
But she is in her grave, and, oh,
The difference to me!

In this poem, Wordsworth references a female child as a connection that children often have to nature. Later research has revealed that "she" is an actual child that Wordsworth knew by the name of Lucy, and he wrote five poems about her in a group of Lucy Poems. In this poem, Lucy exists in a paradise that is free of humanity, for she lives in "untrodden ways," or a place that no one has stepped foot upon before. Wordsworth is making a connection of childhood innocence with nature. Adults often look upon a rainbow as a thing of beauty, but a child sees it as something grand and magical. Children are connected to nature as much as ancient cultures were as seen by their mythology. The only tragedy is that children grow up, become adults, and either forget their connection to nature, or in some way become a part of its destruction. Though this child is dead, and none may know of her, the fact that she has reminded the narrator of humanity's connection with nature is enough to praise her as being part of nature.

Imagery in Poetry

A popular mantra of all writers is "show; don' t tell." This is particularly the case for poets. Their duty is to show us worlds of sight, sound, taste, smell, and touch in exact detail. Thus, we, as readers, need to read not only with our eyes, but with our ears as well. The words in poems create images and feelings that need to be understood on various levels.

An image accurately depicts our senses, emotions, or thoughts in a way that all can understand. We spend most of our days looking at the world through a dirty window pane. Poets are like window washers clearing away our obscure view of the world and even opening the window so that we can sense the world around us with greater clarity. This is the way of poetry, to make the world seem clearer. By doing so, poems may generate memories long forgotten, excite feelings we thought never existed, or sway responses in directions we rarely go.

Poets produce images to create such details in the mind's eye. How would you explain rush hour in a subway station with such clarity that only one sentence is needed? Ezra Pound tried it with his one-sentence poem "In a Station in the Metro."

The apparition[38] of these faces in the crowd;
Petals on a wet, black bough.

Here Pound attempts to capture an experience he had in a Paris subway where, upon exiting the train, he noticed faces

---

38 apparition: (n) appearance

that were beautiful to behold. He suffered for a year over the image, trying to put into words what he experienced. He went from a thirty-line poem to a fifteen-line poem and destroyed both, knowing that they did not capture the portrait-like event that he had observed with such clarity.

What he decided upon is best put into his own words, "In a poem of this sort one is trying to record the precise instant when a thing outward and objective transforms itself, or darts into a thing inward and subjective."[39] When he finished, he managed to produce a photogenic piece of poetry that *showed* us the sensory experience of that day and not just *telling* us. By describing the faces of the crowd as an apparition, there is something ghostly and out of focus of what the speaker is seeing, and those faces are likened to petals on a wet, black branch. What the speaker has seen is something bright, wondrous, and alive, in dark, wet subway stations; something beautiful has grown out of despair.

39 See http;//rpo.library.utoronto.ca/poem/1657.html

MEETING AT NIGHT

Robert Browning (1812-1889)

I.

The grey sea and the long black land;
And the yellow half-moon large and low;
And the startled little waves that leap
In fiery ringlets from their sleep,
As I gain the cove with pushing prow,
And quench its speed I'[40] the slushy sand.

40 i': poetic form of "in"

II.

Then a mile of warm sea-scented beach;
Three fields to cross till a farm appears;
A tap at the pane, the quick sharp scratch
And blue spurt of a lighted match,
And a voice less loud, thro' its joys and fears,
Than the two hearts beating each to each!

On just about every line, Browning creates images describing a man going to meet his lover. He is expert in utilizing the five senses to give a sense of immediacy to the poem. In the first stanza, he uses color that not only paints a picture in the reader's mind, but also creates the mood. The details of the moon reflecting on the ocean is familiar to most, but far from being a static scene, the narrator adds action through the "fiery ringlets" that are the moon' s reflection on the ocean, drawing the viewer's eyes to the "waves that leap," conjuring a joyful, urgent motion to the destination of his lover's house. The speed through which he is sailing is brought to a slow halt as the sailor enters the cove, the front of his boat plying the waves, and it becomes beached in the "slushy sand."

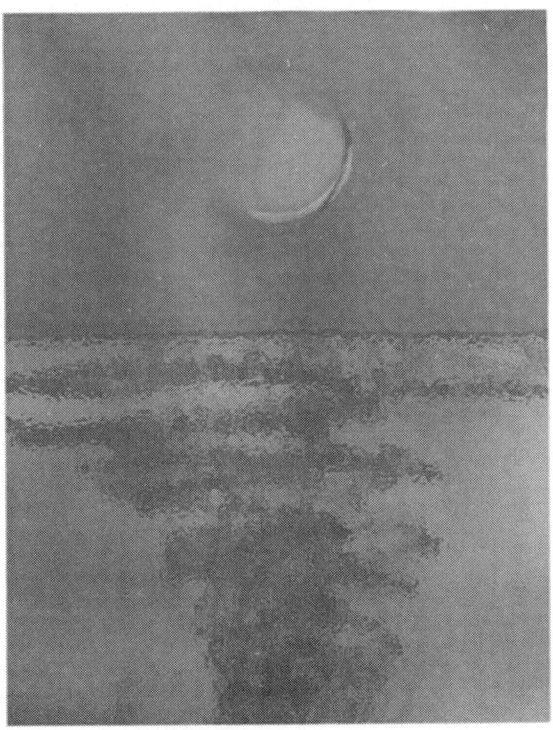

In the second stanza, the sense of smell is awakened through "warm sea-scented beach." He has arrived, and his destination is close. The poem ends with familiar sounds that awaken the mystery and danger of what is going to occur. The sense of sound is highlighted with the sailor tapping on the window pane, followed by the striking and lighting of a match to light the lantern by the lover inside the house. She speaks with a quiet voice full of happiness and fear, perhaps fear of being caught, that is drowned out by the beating of their two hearts. It is interesting that there is no physical description of the woman; she remains a mystery.

Though the two lover's meeting may be in secret and dangerous, their feelings for each other are clear. The journey the sailor takes to meet his lover is no easy task, it would seem, but it is worth it, for the reader goes from the darkness of "the grey sea and the long black land" to the light of the lover's lamp.

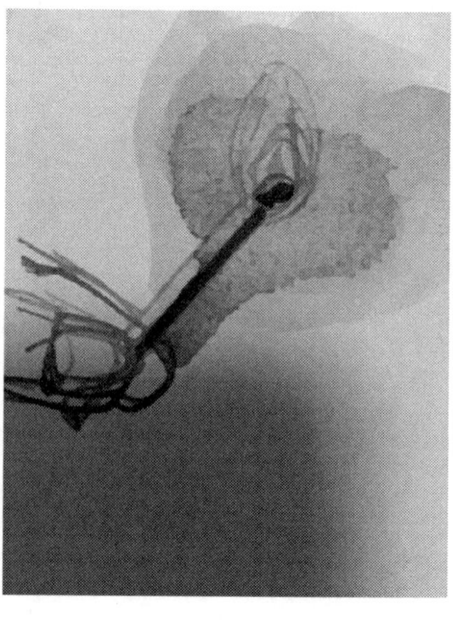

PARTING AT MORNING

Robert Browning

Round the cape of a sudden came the sea,
And the sun looked over the mountain's rim:
And straight was a path of gold for him,
And the need of a world of men for me.

This short poem would seem to be the next day when the sailor leaves his lover with the coming of the tide. It is in stark contrast to the darkness of the previous tryst, while the sun seems bright and golden on this special morning. Though the sailor is leaving, the lover knows he will return, for his path is as straight as the sun's reflection on the ocean.

A Brief Introduction to Robert Browning

An enigmatic figure in his own time, Robert Browning rose from obscurity to become both popular and misunderstood. He was born in London to a bank clerk, who owned an extensive library and made sure his son was well educated. Browning spent most of his youth at home, for unlike other poets of his time, he rarely traveled, thus, enjoying good health. Though he attended a boarding school and later the University of London, he was mostly tutored privately at his home where he read, hungering for knowledge in books.

Imitating Percy Bysshe Shelley's personal style, Browning published his first poem, *Pauline*, by the time he was twenty-one. It received harsh criticism. Many critics accused him of creating a spectacle of "gross vanity." Extremely embarrassed by the attacks, he withdrew into the voice of his characters never to be found again.

Deciding poetry might not be the best way to write, Browning switched to penning plays. He started work on his first drama, a historical tragedy called *Stafford* in 1836, which was produced a year later and only lasted four nights. Browning attempted to succeed with his plays over the next ten years but found little respect in this field as well. From his failure, though, he did find the secret he was looking for to succeed. He excelled with the **dramatic monologue** in his dramas and was often criticized for his characters talking about an action instead of doing it. The dramatic monologue was a way for Browning to write poetic verse through a certain character's point of view without revealing his own thoughts and desires, thus, the ambiguity to Browning's actual stance on many topics.

In 1842, he published his first collection of monologues in *Dramatic Lyrics*. Foremost of the collection is the poem, "My Last Duchess." The poet's voice is hard to find, for it is written from the point of view of the Duke, and it is as if the reader is overhearing a secret conversation where the Duke talks of his dead wife and negotiates his marriage to another. Nevertheless, with this collection, Browning still failed to gather a following.

In 1845, Browning's world and fortunes changed: he was in love. He met Elizabeth Barrett, an infirm lady six years his senior, whose poor health was only to be made worse from the abuse she suffered from her possessive father. Being drawn to her, in part by her excellent poetry, Browning proposed to her. Defying her father, Browning and Barrett eloped to Italy where she regained her full

health, and they lived together in comfort. Most of their memorable love poems were written to each other. Though Browning published a popular set of poems entitled *Men and Women* in 1855, he still hadn't gained the respect he needed or deserved. In fact, many of his critics refer to him as "Mrs. Browning's husband," since Elisabeth was more recognized at the time.

The time for the Brownings in Italy was golden as most of their poetry reflects. They continued to live in peace and comfort when in 1861, Elizabeth, finally succumbing to her ill health, died in her husband's arms. Browning returned to England the same year.

The years that followed, though full of loss over the passing of his wife, were filled with success as Browning finally received recognition for his writing. By 1868, he finally proved that he was a poet beyond station with the publication of his greatest work, *The Ring and the Book*. Reading as a novel in verse form, *The Ring* introduced the idea of various points of view that became popular in later literary works.

Retiring to Venice, Browning died December 12th, 1889. His body was returned to England, and he was buried in Westminster Abbey.

MY LAST DUCHESS

Robert Browning

Ferrara

That's my last duchess painted on the wall,
Looking as if she were alive. I call
That piece a wonder, now: Frà[41] Pandolf's hands

Worked busily a day, and there she stands.
Will't please you sit and look at her? I said
"Frà Pandolf" by design, for never read
Strangers like you that pictured countenance,
The depth and passion of its earnest glance,
But to myself they turned (since none puts by
The curtain I have drawn for you, but I)
And seemed as they would ask me, if they durst[42],
How such a glance came there; so, not the first
Are you to turn and ask thus. Sir, 'twas not
Her husband's presence only, called that spot
Of joy into the Duchess' cheek: perhaps

41 Fra: (n) a friar in the Roman Catholic Church

42 durst: (v) old form meaning 'dared'

Frà Pandolf chanced to say "Her mantle[43] laps[44]
"Over my lady's wrist too much," or "Paint
"Must never hope to reproduce the faint
"Half-flush that dies along her throat": such stuff
Was courtesy, she thought, and cause enough
For calling up that spot of joy. She had
A heart how shall I say? too soon made glad,

Too easily impressed; she liked whate'er
She looked on, and her looks went everywhere.
Sir, 'twas all one! My favor at her breast,
The dropping of the daylight in the West,
The bough of cherries some officious[45] fool
Broke in the orchard for her, the white mule
She rode with round the terrace all and each
Would draw from her alike the approving speech,
Or blush, at least. She thanked men good! but thanked
Somehow I know not how as if she ranked
My gift of a nine-hundred-years-old name
With anybody's gift. Who'd stoop to blame
This sort of trifling? Even had you skill
In speech which I have not to make your will

43 mantle: (n) a cape or cloak

44 lap: (v) to hang over

45 officious: (adj) eager to serve

Quite clear to such an one, and say, "Just this
"Or that in you disgusts me; here you miss,
"Or there exceed the mark" and if she let
Herself be lessoned so, nor plainly set
Her wits to yours, forsooth[46], and make excuse,
E'en then would be some stooping; and I choose
Never to stoop. Oh sir, she smiled, no doubt,
Whene'er I passed her; but who passed without
Much the same smile? This grew; I gave commands;
Then all smiles stopped together. There she stands
As if alive. Will't please you rise? We'll meet
The company below, then. I repeat,
The Count your master's known munificence[47]
Is ample warrant that no just pretense
Of mine for dowry[48] will be disallowed;
Though his fair daughter's self, as I avowed[49]
At starting, is my object. Nay we'll go
Together down, sir. Notice Neptune[50], though,
Taming a sea-horse, thought a rarity,
Which Claus of Innsbruck cast in bronze for me!

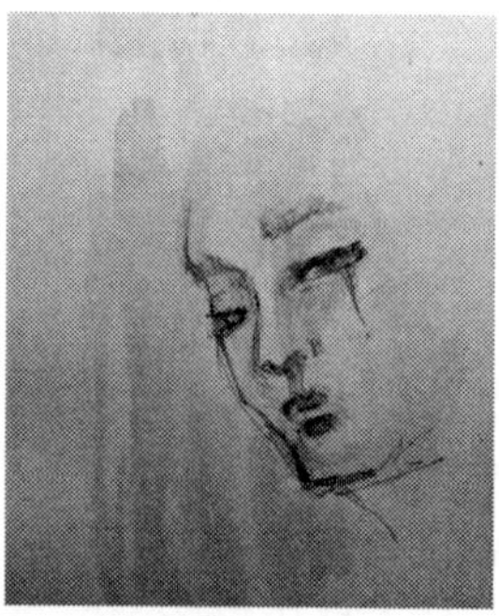

46 forsooth: (adv) old form meaning 'in truth'

47 munificence: (n) generosity

48 dowry: (n) money that the bride's family gives to the groom

49 avow: (v) declare

50 Neptune: (n) Roman god of the sea; Poseidon in Greek

The poem both starts and ends on works of art, the first being a fresco of the narrator's dead wife. Frescos are works of watercolor painted directly on a plaster wall, which contrasts the idea that art and the object of art are both seen as something to possess. The poem reveals the Duke' s controlling nature over his wife, and if he cannot have her in life, he can just as easily own her in death through art.

Possession of art symbolizes some control over the subject matter. Read carefully how he describes the beauty of the painting and compare it with how he feels for his dead wife. The painting is a rather romanticized idea of what his wife should have been—a beautiful, silent creature for him to admire. More interesting is the Duke's own opinion of himself. This poem reads like we are watching a play because it is written as a **dramatic monologue**. Though he is talking about art, it is the information he reveals that becomes the focus of the poem.

Though art is what they are viewing, life is what is revealed. Thus, a beautiful young woman of a lower class but married with a great dowry is found difficult to control. When she is discovered flirting with other men, the Duke gives "commands" and has her killed. However, he feels no remorse because there is another woman with a large dowry to pursue.

It just so happens that the person he is talking to is an emissary for another Duke looking to give his daughter away for marriage. Finally, at the end of the poem, we see the second work of art, a bronze statue of Neptune taming a sea-horse. Again, the Duke's psyche is revealed through a work of art, mainly that he sees himself as Neptune and women as the sea-horse.

The Golden Age of Literature

After the death of Queen Elizabeth I in 1603, her cousin James I of Scotland became King. It was a peaceful succession without any bloodshed, coups, or rebellions. There were two failed assassination attempts against him and his family during his reign, however. He was not English. He was Scottish, and his queen was from Denmark. Many feared he would threaten English interests and traditions, but he did unify England and Scotland. He was considered dangerous because he thought the king was a god on Earth and ruled by divine authority. This did not make the Parliament feel very comfortable. In fact, it led to James basically ignoring Parliament for long periods of time and only calling on them when the monarchy needed money.

James I, like Elizabeth, was a patron of the arts and continued the "Golden Age" of Literature. This is called the Jacobean Age (1603-1625), Jacobus being the Latin name of James. The court system of sponsorship continued under his reign as well as his son, Charles I. Most of the poets at this time were courtiers and had to be seen at court to be known and for their works to be circulated. During this time, both poetry and prose were becoming the main form of artistic expression in the English language. The Jacobean era also introduced the essay as a new genre of prose, brought to England by Francis Bacon. Shakespeare continued to flourish in the theater, writing his greatest tragedies and romances during this period. Poets and writers, such as Ben Jonson and John Donne also rose to prominence during his reign.

ON MY FIRST SON

Ben Jonson (1572-1637)

Farewell, thou child of my right hand, and joy;
        My sin was too much hope of thee, loved boy.
Seven years thou wert[51] lent to me, and I thee pay.
        Exacted by the fate, on the just day.
Oh, could I lose all father now! For why
        Will man lament the state he should envy?
To have so soon 'scaped[52] world's and flesh's rage,
        And, if no other misery, yet age?
Rest in soft peace, and asked, say here doth lie
        Ben Jonson his best piece of poetry;
For whose sake, henceforth, all his vows be such,
        As what he loves may never like too much.

51 wert: (v) old form meaning 'was'

52 'scaped: (v) escaped; to fit the meter the poet cut off the first syllable

"On My First Son" is a great example of an **elegy**, a thoughtful poem that laments the dead. Jonson wrote it after the death of his son in 1603 due to the Bubonic Plague. This is one of the rare occasions when the speaker of a poem and poet are the same. This is known as the **autobiographical "I"**.

Before Jonson wrote this poem, he spoke of a bizarre dream where he visited his friend Sir Robert Cotton. He recounted the dream to William Drummond, a man whom he stayed with during a walking tour of England with a friend, Mr. Camden. Drummond writes what Jonson told him. "He saw in a vision his eldest son (then a child and at London) appear unto him with the mark of a bloody cross on his forehead, as if it had been cutted with a sword, at which amazed, he prayed unto God, and in the morning he came to Mr. Camden's chamber to tell him, who persuaded him it was but an apprehension of his fantasy at which he should not be disjected[53]; in the meantime comes there letters from his wife of the death of that boy in the plague. He appeared to him (he said) of a manly shape, and of that growth that he thinks he shall be at the resurrection."

Jonson wrote this elegy using several classical **epigrams**, which are short, balanced, and elegant sayings made popular during ancient Greece, especially by Martial (40-104). Jonson was the most proficient writer of epigrams in the English language, and he uses this knowledge to the maximum in this poem. Every two lines consist of an epigram. In fact, his final epigram, "For whose sake, henceforth, all his vows be such, / As what he loves may never like too much," subtly echoes a famous one by Martial, "Whatever you love, may you wish not to have been overly pleased by it" (VI.xxix). Since it was written in English, Jonson's epigram has a more poetic ring to it.

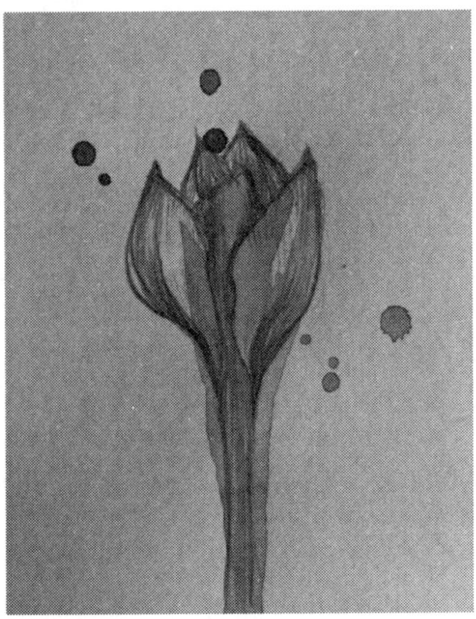

53 disjected: (v) old form of dejected, or sad

A Brief Introduction to Ben Jonson

As one of the first well-rounded English men of letters, Ben Jonson was adopted at a young age by a bricklayer after his father's untimely death. Though not raised with wealth, Jonson received a grand education at the tutelage of a great classical scholar, William Camden. In his early twenties, Jonson entered the army and fought against the Spaniards. He then returned to England to begin his life as an actor in 1595. He would go on to be an accomplished playwright, poet, scholar, critic, translator, poet laureate for the King, and the first founder of a literary school in England.

Not that Jonson was destined for such a station; he was first a man of action. He was imprisoned for a time for killing a fellow actor in a duel. Only his ability to read and write Latin saved him from the death penalty. He had another brush with the law when he served time in jail for insulting the Scottish shortly after King James I, a Scottish

King, took the crown. And to add insult to injury, he converted to Catholicism in a country stoutly Protestant. However, his great talent for language and writing brought him early fame and notoriety.

Already good friends with William Shakespeare and John Donne, Jonson took younger writers of talent and guided them to great success. Together, they started the Cavalier school of English poets that rivaled John Donne' s metaphysical poets. These new young poets dubbed themselves "Sons of Ben".

Starting as an actor/playwright, Jonson's first great play was *Every Man in his Humor* (1598), written for the Lord Chamberlain's Men with Shakespeare as the lead actor. Jonson followed this with his two great satire comedies, *Volpone* (1606) and *The Alchemist* (1610).

Jonson, like Shakespeare, also wrote successful poetry. Falling into five stylistic groups, his first poetic style is festive ceremony poems celebrating the good life. "To Penhurst" is a good example of celebrating the life of the countryside. Second are his elegies and epitaphs that were short, simple poems often meant to be carved on tombstones, such as "On My First Son".

Close to the elegies are his compliments and tributes written for the character and achievements of people he knew and respected. "To the Memory of My Beloved Master William Shakespeare" (1616) is a good example of this. Last of Jonson's stylistic groups are epigrams written in imitation of the romantic poet Martial. They are vulgar, nasty, and sometimes funny poems that were a style seen to revolt against Elizabethan romanticism.

In 1616 King James I appointed Jonson as poet laureate. Soon after, Jonson became the first English writer to ever publish a collection of his own works, titled *The Works of Benjamin Jonson.*

The Victorian Age
(1830-1901)

In 1811, King George III was declared incurably insane. His eldest son, the Prince of Wales, was made regent, and upon the king's death in 1820, he ruled as George IV. When George IV died in 1830, his brother William IV became King. Having no legitimate heirs, William IV was succeeded by his niece Victoria upon his death in 1837. However, the Victorian Age started in 1832 with the passing of the Reform Bill that allowed the middle class to vote and to keep any political and economic power created through the Industrial Revolution. This allowed England to become the greatest economic power in the world. During the Romantic period, London housed a mere two million people. Near the end of the Victorian Age, London boasted over 6.5 million people.

As the first industrial nation, the English suffered through swift and horrible change. The rich and the middle class prospered as their country traded with and dominated many countries in their expanding empire, while the lower class was forced into economic squalor and inhumane living conditions. The writing of this age characterized societal confusion, the discrimination of the rich against the poor, the base conditions many were forced to live in, and the glory of England's longest-ruling monarch, Queen Victoria.

A Brief Introduction to Gerard Manley Hopkins

(1844-1889)

Gerard Manley Hopkins was a minor poet of the Victorian Age, who produced a small body of poems which were never published during his lifetime, yet his influence was great upon 20th century poets.

His family was wealthy and highly artistic, so he ultimately studied the classics at Balliol College at Oxford, where he became deeply involved in religious reform and was influenced by the Oxford Movement that began in 1833. Many of these supporters, including Hopkins, went from the Church of England and converted to the Roman Catholic Church in 1866 due to the religious controversy and confusion the movement stirred. Upon entering the society of Jesus, or the Jesuits, in 1868, Hopkins was ordained a priest two years later, whereupon he dedicated the rest of his life to his religion. Already showing great promise as a poet, Hopkins burnt all the poetry he had written up to

that point, for he saw the line between religion and aesthetics as a dividing factor for a priest, and he would never pen another poem until 1875 after wrestling with spiritual depression.

Not until Hopkins called his spiritual life into question did he begin to write again. Feeling the religious bareness that accompanies a spiritual's quest for the divine, Hopkins often felt dejected and started writing to deal with the doubt he often felt. His first poem, "The Wreck of the Deutschland", was in memory of the five Franciscan nuns exiled from Germany who drowned when their ship sank in the mouth of the Thames. He continued to write his greatest works after that, including "God's Grandeur."

GOD'S GRANDEUR

Gerard Manley Hopkins

The World is charged with the grandeur of God.
It will flame out, like shining from shook foil;
It gathers to a greatness, like the ooze of oil
Crushed. Why do men then now not reck[54] his rod?[55]
Generations have trod, have trod, have trod;
And all is seared with trade; bleared, smeared with toil;
And wears man's smudge and shares man's smell: the soil
Is bare now, nor can foot feel, being shod.[56]

And for all this, nature is never spent;
There lives the dearest freshness deep down things;
And though the last lights off the black West went
Oh, morning, at the brown brink eastward, springs—
Because the Holy Ghost[57] over the bent
World broods with warm breast and with ah! bright
wings.

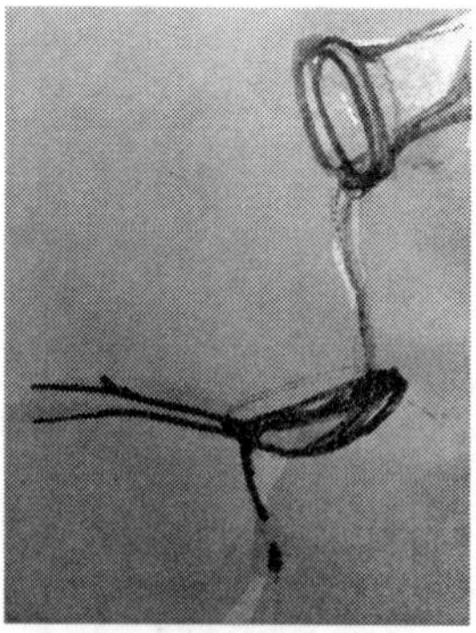

54 reck: (v) old form meaning 'to have regard for' or 'to obey'

55 rod: (n) a stick of authority (God's authority)

56 shod: (adj) provided with shoes

57 Holy Ghost: the holy spirit of the Trinity (Godhead): God the father, Jesus, the son, and the holy spirit;

The world would be fallen if not for "the grandeur of God." Hopkins utilizes **alliteration** throughout the poem to illustrate this divine connection with God, such as **consonance**: "**G**randeur of **G**od", "**sh**ining from **sh**ook foil", "**g**athers to a **g**reatness," and **assonance**: "the **oo**ze of **o**il." The closeness of the words and sound reminds us of the intimacy of God as does the stern tone of the narrator simulating a church sermon. As we read each line, the alternation from harsh consonance to light **sibilance** indicates the harshness of the sinner offset by the grace of God. Though the world is bathed in God's divine grace, humanity wallows in the filth below, ignoring all that God has given, labeled here as the grandeur.

The second stanza gives us the sense that as fallen beings, we have somehow trampled the divine earth under foot, and through disreputable work, we have surrounded ourselves with unnatural works of our hands, "all is seared with trade," being cut off from the natural world of God. There is even a sense of the industrial cities "bleared, smeared with toil" soiling the divinity of humanity.

Though all seems lost, it is not so, for the morning brings the "dearest freshness". As the day sloughs off the darkness in the west, the light in the east rises. We may continue to destroy the earth, but God will always be there, "for all this, nature is never spent." Equally, we may sin and toil a while in darkness, but God will always be there, like the sun in the morning, to forgive us through the Holy Ghost. The use of "ah," adds reassurance from the narrator that all is well, and no matter how dark the night was, God will be there in the morning with "bright wings."

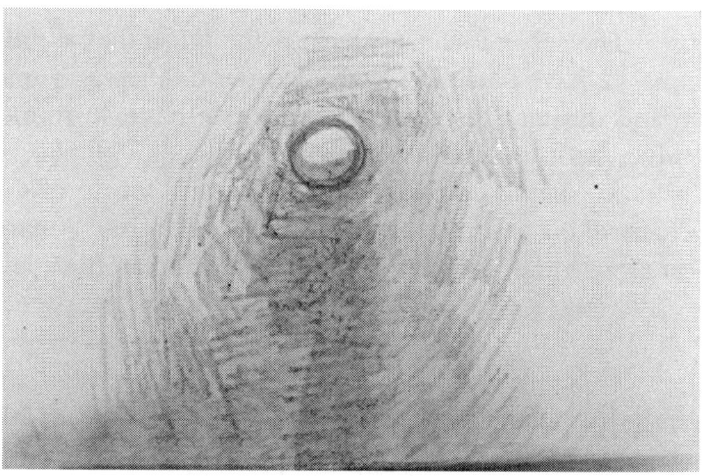

THEME TWO: PERSONAL IDENTITY

The following poems explore the circumstances under which a person at one time in life is still the same person at another time even though appearances change. Human life has basically been separated into three stages: youth, middle age, and old age. To the youth, the elderly appear to be from a different time, a different age, even alien, but do the youth ever sit back and think what they will be like when they are older?

Poems about personal identity are deeply contemplative and often self-assessing. Such poetry can be viewed as confessional, written with honest self-definition and revelation. Personal identity poetry showcases how the poets use their language to express powerful emotion. Perhaps you as the reader can turn the poet's voice inward and discover something new and wonderous about your own life and identity.

If any poet had mastered the deeply contemplative form of poetry, it was William Wordsworth. By 1799, Wordsworth moved to the Lake District where he entered the spring of his writing career. He published the two most popular editions of poems: *Poems in Two Volumes* (1807) and *The Excursion* (1814). Most of his memorable poetry comes from these two editions. The genius of Wordsworth was his ability to revisit a time in the past and add a new perspective to it. He would return to the scene in his mind where he witnessed something as a youth but add a fresh mature perspective to it again, as in his poem "I Wander Lonely as a Cloud." "Lines Composed a Few Miles Above Tintern Abbey" was the concluding poem to *Lyrical Bal-*

lads and was written well after a walking tour he took in South Wales. Other poems were composed after contemplation upon certain subjects, as with "A Slumber Did My Spirit Seal," which is a meditation upon the death of a loved one; Coleridge suspected it was an epitaph written for Wordsworth's sister after a fit of depression found him thinking upon his sister's future death.

RAINBOW

William Wordsworth (1770-1850)

My heart leaps up when I behold
A rainbow in the sky:
So was it when my life began;
So is it now I am a man;
So be it when I shall grow old,
Or let me die!
The Child is father of the Man;
I could wish my days to be
Bound each to each by natural piety.

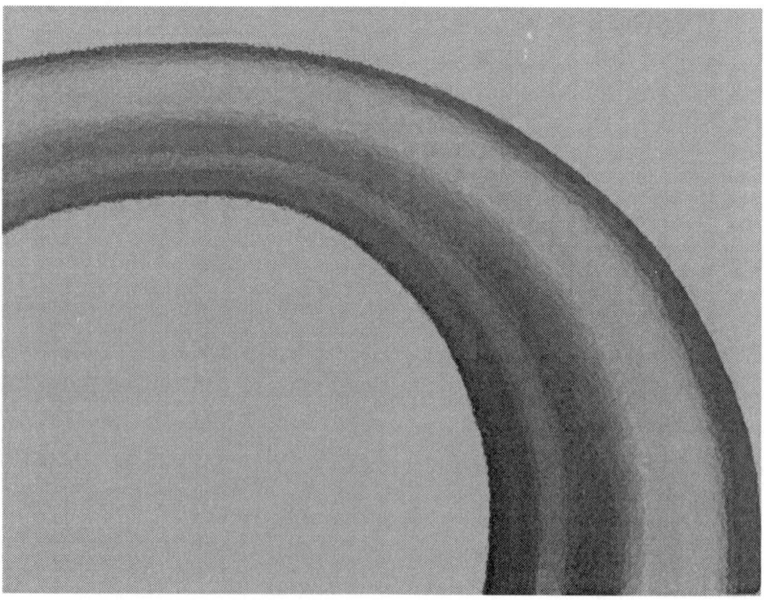

Although a rather simple poem, "Rainbow", like most of his later poems, is full of **paradox**. The line, "The Child is father of the Man" may appear as a paradox. Obviously, a child cannot be a father of a man. However, upon a second reading—and understanding Wordsworth' s history—we can see that the narrator views his past self as a child who then becomes the father of his present self, the man he will become. It is not a literal meaning, but a **metaphor**. The younger self existed before the older self, and his experiences give birth to the older identity. We are all like this. We are shaped or formed by our previous experiences, meaning that our younger selves are the teachers or elders of our current personalities.

Wordsworth also implies that the adult can learn from his or her younger self. When the narrator was young, he was fascinated by nature's beauty such as rainbows. Now that he is older, the image of a rainbow still holds awe for him. He remembers what it was like to experience a rainbow as a child and hopes that this awe will continue into his old age. One must not forget how the child experiences life.

In Wordsworth's later years, his poetry declined because of the way he wrote. His greatest poetry was a mature man living in comfort looking back upon times of youth full of doubt and adventures. In other words, he is sitting in peace and calm looking back upon emotion and agony. Near the end of his life, he was an experienced poet, a retired recluse, looking back upon a life of calm and comfort. Not much in his later life sparked the emotion and wit like in his youth. In 1843, he was awarded poet laureate after he denounced his radical French sympathies.

A Brief Introduction to William Blake

(1757-1827)

Though William Blake was not recognized as a Romantic poet until well after the Big Five had been established, he still promoted the ideals that made the period so vibrant and was later included to be part of the **Big Six**. Blake was devoutly religious as a youth and never had a formal education forced upon him. As he grew older, Blake read the classics to further his own education.

Always an imaginative child, Blake often spoke of a religious vision he had as a child of eight, where he saw a tree covered with angels. He was educated in the trade as an artist when he apprenticed as an engraver. He was sent to Westminster Abby to sketch many of the monuments there. While in this holy place, he claimed to have had a full vision of Christ and the apostles. As he grew older, he became disillusioned with the institutionalization of religion, but he always remained a spiritual person. While writing his **epic** poem *Milton* (1804), Blake claimed that he composed it while in a waking dream, dictated by Milton himself. Blake also hated what the Industrial Revolution had turned humanity into. Factories, machines, and analytical science were the causes of England's spiritual despair. What he hated was how humanity had embraced the unthinking precision of science at the cost of imagination and humanity.

Blake started his literary career as a poet. Between the ages of twelve and twenty, he printed *Poetical Sketches* (1783). Though not his best work, it does show his desire to break away from the neoclassical style by going back to a more Elizabethan one. The most accessible of his poetry are the two volumes called *Songs of Innocence* (1789) and *Songs of Experience* (1794). They contrast the conflicting reality of human nature, and without these contraries, humanity could not learn, progress, or even know God. For God, in Blake's mind, was a contrary Being; one who gave both mercy and judgment, who loved the sinner but hated sin. The innocent poem "The Lamb" and the experience poem "The Tyger" demonstrate the contrary character of nature, and they are great examples of Blake mixing imagination with nature that the Romantics were so skillful with. Here are the first six lines of both poems:

The Lamb
Little Lamb, who made thee?
Dost though know who made thee?
Gave thee life, and bid thee feed,
By the stream and o'er the mead;
Gave thee clothing of delight,
Softest clothing, wool bright,

The Tyger
Tyger! Tyger! burning bright
In the forests of the night,
What immortal hand or eye
Could frame thy fearful symmetry?
In the distant deeps or skies
Burnt the fires of thine eyes?

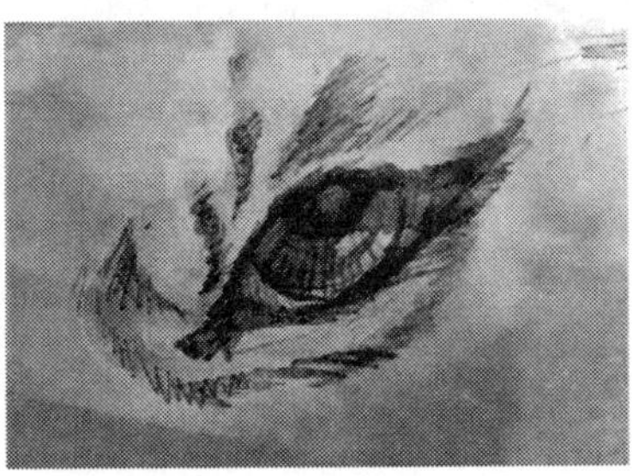

The innocent lamb represents not only Christ, but also the innocence of children and nature. The fiery tiger is nature deformed after scientific and industrial corruption. It represents a Milton-like Satan as well as the jaded view of adulthood.

Blake was expert at symbolism and created a whole new mythology of symbols to hide the revolutionary content of his writing so as not to enrage the political establishment. When the Reign of Terror took over the French Revolution, Blake took a step back from his revolutionary writing and started to hide his political revolutionary passion behind a more inner spiritual revolution. As he got older, Blake's symbolism became more eccentric and difficult to interpret. However, his early poetry is still full of symbolism. A good example of this is from another poem of experience "A Poison Tree."

A POISON TREE

William Blake

I was angry with my friend:
I told my wrath, my wrath did end.
I was angry with my foe;
I told it not, my wrath did grow.

And I watered it in fears,
Night & morning with my tears;
And I sunnèd it with my smiles
And with soft deceitful wiles[58].

And it grew both day and night,
Till it bore an apple bright;
And my foe beheld it shine,
And he knew that it was mine,

And into my garden stole
When the night had veiled the pole:
In the morning glad I see
My foe outstretched beneath the tree

58 wile: (n) trickery

William Blake gives a radical view of how a person reacts to another who has encroached upon his own personal space. The narrator is angry with both a friend and an enemy. When he expresses his anger to his friend, the rift is healed, and his anger ends. But he hides his anger from his enemy, an anger that grows into a tree that yields a poisonous fruit upon which his enemy will eat and die from. This simple poem expresses the complex hypocritical duality we all hold within our psyche. What is often a tragedy of human life is the fact that anger is suppressed by hate. Anger is a healthy way of dealing with those who have wronged us. Hate is unhealthy, for, like the poem, it is secret and destructive not only to those who are hated but to the hater as well. While the hater shrivels up inside and becomes bitter and loathing, the object of that hate continues, oblivious to the hate. When both meet, the hater smiles and talks nicely, and then curses that same person behind his or her back. Thus, by the end of the poem, when the object of that hate lies dead, the hater feels victorious. But victory is never achieved out of hate. There are no winners, and, as this poem stresses, both suffer enormously in the end.

A Brief Introduction of Emily Dickinson

(1830-1886)

Emily Dickinson was a New England poet who wrote during the American Civil War, yet there is never any mention of the conflict in her works. Her writing was extremely personal. She was an agoraphobic, and never left her house. Being shut in her house gave her a better perspective of the quiet inner workings of the soul that many writers of the industrialized 19th century had missed. As a woman, she had nothing but time to think and contemplate about the soul. She wrote more than 2,000 poems but only published seven anonymously. Not that this small number of publications was of her choosing. She tried, and many refused to publish her poetry. Thus, she had very little influence during her lifetime. Unlike her contemporary Walt Whitman, who created the expansive epic of American poetry, Dickinson turned inward to the tragic and philosophical side of the American psyche.

The rejection of Dickinson's poetry should not be seen as a fault of what she was writing. She was just ahead of her time in terms of style and content. Like Whitman, she refused to write the way everyone else was writing, especially like the English. Her poems did not rhyme and were not formatted in a traditional way; she loved to use dashes to jar the reader from smooth traditional rhythms. She also did not use commas, semicolons, or periods. In other words, her poetry did not use conventional poetic sentences. Another problem was that no one could understand her **figures of speech**; they were too drastic, and her ideas were too extreme, especially from a woman!

Dickinson was raised in a Calvinist household but later rejected her religious upbringing. She did keep her thirst for truth and many of her poems are a quest for faith though she never did find any answer to the faith problem. She seems to have multiple answers in her poems as to what faith really is. Though the Bible was a major influence on her thinking, she often turned to Ralph Waldo Emerson for philosophical inspiration, especially his work *Self-Reliance*. Much of her writing could be classified as Transcendental as well, for she often looked at the potential of humanity instead of the reality. Thus, the images and themes that occupy her mind are mostly lifted from Emerson's essays, but she presented them through her own stimulating point of view. She went where Emerson never even thought to go with his philosophy: examining suffering, limitations, and death. Perhaps this is because in a three-year period, thirty-three of her friends and family members had passed away.

After Dickinson's own death, her sister found most of her poems and tried to arrange them into booklets that followed a theme, such as death, nature, and love. There was a small following of these booklets, but many critics complained that Dickinson did not understand what poetry was; thus, editors made changes to the poems to fit the poetic tastes of the times. Not until 1955 did Dickinson's original poems start to gather a following when all her poems were published in order of creation. The reading public was just not ready for her until such a time. She is absolutely modern, and if she had lived in the mid-20th century, she would have been a great success. To understand how truly out of her time she really was, let's analyze one of her famous poems "Because I Could Not Stop for Death."

BECAUSE I COULD NOT STOP FOR DEATH

Emily Dickinson

Because I could not stop for Death—
He kindly stopped for me—
The Carriage[59] held but just Ourselves—
And Immortality.

We slowly drove—He knew no haste
And I had put away
My labor and my leisure too,
For His Civility—

We passed the School, where Children strove
At Recess—in the Ring—
We passed the Fields of Gazing Grain—
We passed the Setting Sun—

59 Carriage: hearse

Or rather—He passed Us—
The Dews drew quivering and chill—
For only Gossamer,[60] my Gown—
My Tippet[61]—only Tulle[62]—

We paused before a House that seemed
A Swelling of the Ground—
The Roof was scarcely visible—
The Cornice[63]—in the Ground—

Since then—'tis Centuries—and yet
Feels shorter than the Day
I first surmised the Horses' Heads
Were toward Eternity—

60 Gossamer: (n) a thin, lightweight material

61 Tippet: (n) scarf

62 Tulle: a thin, silk material woven into a net

63 Cornice: (n) a stone molding surrounding a roof

This poem shows the narrator's fear of death, yet there is a beauty to it that is normally not associated with death and funerals. The first stanza explains that the narrator did not want to die; she uses a carriage as a **metaphor** for death that carries her away. The journey is slow, and she can only observe. She feels like she is moving, but it is life that is moving on; this is the first time in her "life" she has ever had time, for death makes time for all. The fourth stanza describes the death shroud she is dressed in (her gossamer gown), and the fifth stanza describes the house that is "a swelling of the ground," the tomb where she will live for eternity. Here, in death, time has no meaning, and centuries feel like minutes. Though the narrator is dead, there is no fear in her words, only peace.

Notice how the poem does not have any punctuation outside of the dashes. The lack of rhyme was disconcerting for the 19th century reader, but she does use **slant rhymes**, or half rhymes. In the last stanza, the second and fourth lines end with "Day" and "Eternity." They do not perfectly rhyme, but they do create a slant rhyme through the similarity of end vowels. The first and third lines end with "yet" and "Heads." They do not end rhyme, but they do have **assonance**, where the vowels rhyme. Both "yet" and "Heads" have a short vowel sound that rhymes. This was the problem for both Whitman and Dickinson; their poetry did not rhyme in a time when all poetry had to. If they did not rhyme, the critics did not know how to classify them; they could not possibly be poems!

The **figures of speech** found in this poem, as well as her others, were unusual. Her personification of death as a civil being probably was too liberal at a time of great death and destruction from the Civil War, while her overt fascination with death and the peacefulness of it was far from the common sentimentality of 19th century poetry. What set Dickinson apart from other Civil War poets is that for her, suffering is something that occurs alone. The whole country may be in an upheaval, but the individual must come to terms with such suffering alone at night in "a place where God and nature are silent."

Another form of personal identity is art as an extension of the creative self. Those who create for art's sake and not for money or fame view their creations as a part of themselves that does not belong to anybody else. In fact, nobody can really understand the creation better than the creator. W.B. Yeats's "A Coat" explores this idea of art as a coat he has created.

A COAT

W.B. Yeats (1865-1939)

I made my song a coat
Covered with embroideries
Out of old mythologies
From heel to throat;
But the fools caught it,
Wore it in the world's eyes
As though they'd wrought it.
Song, let them take it,
For there's more enterprise
In walking naked.

Yeats uses the **metaphor** that his creation fits him as a coat and the embroidery that makes it beautiful has been crafted out of moments from his past that he can readily identify with.

However, when others come along and take his coat, which he has put a lot of time and effort into so that it looks appealing, they wear it and show it off as if they were special. This is like academics who sit around all day quoting their favorite poets, sounding important and learned, but have done nothing creative themselves. It is even similar to when we sing famous songs of our favorite pop artists, showing our prowess with a song that is, in fact, not our own. We have created nothing, and yet many envy our skill at wearing another's beautiful coat.

Yeats says, however, to let these people have the coat. It shows their own uncreativeness, while he would rather go naked, for there is more complication and risk in the very act of not creating. Such an act would eventually equal out where all then would have to go naked, having no skill to make their own coat, yet the artist remains an artist, while everyone else is just naked!

Furthermore, the resentment in the poem is handled rather lightly and jokingly. There is no form of malice toward the unartistic who parade around with his ideas. In fact, the narrator seems almost forgiving.

In the next poem, John Milton reminds us how fast time catches up and is the "subtle thief of youth."

HOW SOON HATH TIME

John Milton (1608-1674)

How soon hath Time, the subtle thief of youth,
Stol'n[64] on his wing my three and twentieth year!

My hasting days fly on with full career,
But my late spring no bud or blossom shew'th.
Perhaps my semblance[65] might deceive the truth,
That I to manhood am arrived so near,
And inward ripeness doth much less appear,

64 stole: (v) past tense, to move quietly into a place

65 semblance: (n) the outward appearance

That some more timely-happy spirits endu'th[66].
Yet be it less or more, or soon or slow,
It shall be still in strictest measure even
To that same lot, however mean or high,
Toward which Time leads me, and the will of Heaven;
All is, if I have grace to use it so,
As ever in my great Taskmaster's[67] eye.

66 endu'th: (v) endure

67 Taskmaster: (n) God

The narrator is in his sixties and feels that he has nothing to show at the start of his golden years. He bemoans the fact that his outward appearance cannot possibly show his feelings about how he feels just reaching old age. Though he may be judged to be beyond worth, God can only judge that, so he will accomplish what is ever needed and whatever fate has in store for him.

This type of poem echoes what the philosopher John Locke (1632-1704) would later clarify as consciousness that is the foundation of personal identity and not the body. Since we all will reach the phase of old age sooner or later, we need to judge a person's worth by what this very identity is and not by age or outer appearance.

An individual's personal identity can be defined through a group or organization. As was noted earlier, Protestants were persecuted in England by Catholics during Milton's time. Milton understood how his own identity as a devout Protestant was formed by being part of persecuted group. He wrote of his indignation, as well as other Protestants' throughout England and Europe, toward the Catholic slaughter of the Waldensians in 1655.

ON THE LATE MASSACRE IN PIEDMONT

John Milton

Avenge, O Lord, thy slaughtered saints, whose bones
Lie scattered on the Alpine mountains cold,
Even them who kept thy truth so pure of old
When all our fathers worshiped stocks and stones;
Forget not: in thy book[68] record their groans

Who were thy sheep and in their ancient fold
Slain by the bloody Piedmontese that rolled
Mother with infant down the rocks. Their moans

68 The Book of Life

The vales redoubled to the hills, and they
To Heaven. Their martyred blood and ashes sow
O'er all th' Italian fields where still doth sway

The triple tyrant[69]; that from these may grow
A hundred-fold, who having learnt thy way
Early may fly the Babylonian woe.

69 The Pope who wears a triple crown on his Papal Tiara, no longer worn today

The Waldensians were founded around 1173, and considered heretics by the Catholic Church. By the twelfth century, they were offered Piedmont, a region in northern Italy, to be a place of safety from Catholic persecution. Though it angered the Pope at the time (referred to as the triple tyrant in the poem), they lived in peace. By the Reformation in the sixteenth century, they were thought to be safe from any persecution. With the head of the Catholic Church in Rome, having a whole region of "heretics" in the same country was shameful to many. Eventually, the persecution turned to an all-out massacre as the region was purged of any dissenter. Survivors fled to the Alps and into Switzerland, being chased all the way. Large groups of stragglers were trapped in caves and suffocated as huge fires were built at the entrance with the smoke fanned inside. The women and children who survived the initial purge were also hounded in the mountains, and, when caught, both mother and child were thrown off the cliffs.

THEME THREE: SOLITUDE

Solitude as a word carries negative connotations. We often think that being alone is a form of punishment. That may be true for long-term isolation, but we often value short-term seclusion when we need a break from work or other people. We often seek physical solitude to remove any form of interference to think more clearly or even meditate. Mental solitude is the state we reach when we no longer need to isolate ourselves from the world but can turn inward with high levels of concentration. Regardless of how we find inner quiet, solitude is an important part of the arts, and this section showcases various poets' opinions on the very idea of solitude itself.

DAFFODILS

William Wordsworth (1770-1850)

I wandered lonely as a cloud
That floats on high o'er vales and hills,
When all at once I saw a crowd,
A host, of golden daffodils;
Beside the lake, beneath the trees,
Fluttering and dancing in the breeze.

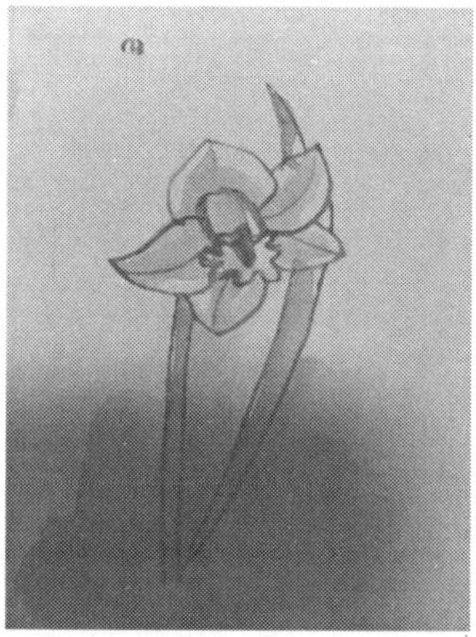

Continuous as the stars that shine
And twinkle on the milky way,
They stretched in never-ending line
Along the margin of a bay:
Ten thousand saw I at a glance,
Tossing their heads in sprightly dance.

The waves beside them danced; but they
Out-did the sparkling waves in glee:

A poet could not but be gay,
In such a jocund[70] company:
I gazed - and gazed - but little thought
What wealth the show to me had brought:

For oft, when on my couch I lie
In vacant or in pensive mood,
They flash upon that inward eye
Which is the bliss of solitude;
And then my heart with pleasure fills,
And dances with the daffodils.

70 jocund: (adj) cheerful

William Wordsworth tried to define poetry as "the spontaneous overflow of powerful feelings…recollected in tranquility." However, if you have ever tried to compose poetry, it is far from spontaneous, and even the best poets take years to refine their poems that have become classics today. The result of such creative outbursts of words on a blank page can be compared to some of the best works of art ever produced on canvas. Wordsworth's poem "Daffodils" can be compared with several of Claude Monet's paintings, especially "Field of Corn"[71] and "Tree"[72]. In fact, Wordsworth said of this poem that it was his intention to bring the power and beauty of a poem to the middle and lower classes without it losing any merit. This poem could be displayed in a museum next to works of art by Monet and Van Gogh, for the enjoyment of art is not in the casual glancing at a picture but a long thoughtful study of the medium, and, in this sense, the words and how they create such a wondrous picture in our minds and a tranquil feeling in our soul.

71 http://www.canvaz.com/gallery/754.htm

72 http://www.canvaz.com/gallery/38.htm

A Brief Introduction of William Butler Yeats

(1865-1939)

Considered one of the greatest English poets of the 20th century, William Butler Yeats was born in Dublin, Ireland. W.B. Yeats's family moved to London in 1874 where he attended school. After his graduation from high school in 1883, Yeats decided to become an artist and to write poetry as a hobby. He entered the Metropolitan School of Art where he met George Russell, a poet, dramatist, and painter, who became an early influence on Yeats's interest in mysticism and the occult. He eventually left art to concentrate fully on his poetry, and moving back to Dublin in 1883, he published his first poem two years later in the *Dublin University Review*. With his interest in the occult as strong as ever, he established the Dublin Lodge of the Hermetic Society in 1886. This marked the first of two phases in Yeats' writing, which was highly influenced by Percy Shelley and Edmund Spencer, utilizing Irish mythology as his subject matter and the revitalization of Celtic consciousness. 1888 and 1892 saw the publication of two mythological editions,

Fairy and Folk Tales of the Irish Peasantry and *Irish Fairy Tales*, while he wrote his own mythological poems based on Irish legend and published them in a collection called *The Wanderings of Oisen and Other Poems* (1889). *Oisen* was his last attempt of an epic style poem; he turned to shorter verse, which contains more of his potent imagery.

Perhaps the dividing line between the mystical writings of Yeats's youth and the mature, down to earth writings of his adulthood is the influence of World War I. The passing of this great war clearly marked the division of the two sides of Yeats. The second phase of Yeats's poetry is more mature and straightforward as he distanced himself from his mystic youth. The themes he started to tackle were the struggles between the material and spiritual world, as well as reality and the imagination. These poems mark him as a great 20th century poet. Mixing with other literary figures such as Ezra Pound, Oscar Wilde, Virginia Woolf, and T. S. Eliot, Yeats saw the need to bring Irish literature to the fore as much as English literature had done. He wrote some of his greatest poetry after the War, including "The

Second Coming" (1920), "The Tower" (1925), and "Sailing to Byzantium (1927).

As a poet, dramatist, mystic, and father of modern Irish literature, Yeats received the Nobel Prize for literature in 1923. In his final years, Yeats suffered from severe illness and later died while in France in 1939, just eight months before World War II plunged the world into another cycle of chaos.

SAILING TO BYZANTIUM[73]

William Butler Yeats

I

That is no country for old men. The young
In one another's arms, birds in the trees
—Those dying generations—at their song,
The salmon-falls,[74] the mackerel-crowded seas,

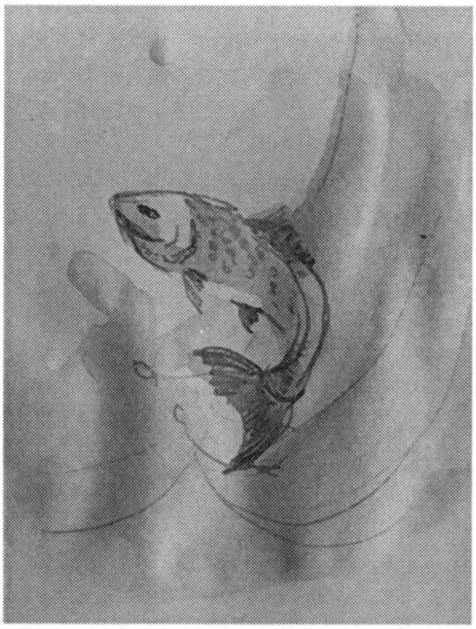

Fish, flesh, or fowl, commend all summer long
Whatever is begotten, born, and dies.
Caught in that sensual music all neglect
Monuments of unageing intellect.

73 Byzantium: an ancient Greek city that was rebuilt by Constantine in 330 and renamed Constantinople (modern day Istanbul, Turkey), the New Rome that became the largest and wealthiest city in the Middle Ages

74 salmon-falls: referencing how salmon swim up river, even up small waterfalls, to spawn

II

An aged man is but a paltry[75] thing,
A tattered coat upon a stick, unless
Soul clap its hands and sing, and louder sing
For every tatter in its mortal dress,
Nor is there singing school but studying
Monuments of its own magnificence;
And therefore I have sailed the seas and come
To the holy city of Byzantium.

75 paltry: (adj) worthless

III

O sages standing in God's holy fire
As in the gold mosaic[76] of a wall,
Come from the holy fire, perne in a gyre,[77]
And be the singing-masters of my soul.
Consume my heart away; sick with desire
And fastened to a dying animal
It knows not what it is; and gather me
Into the artifice of eternity.

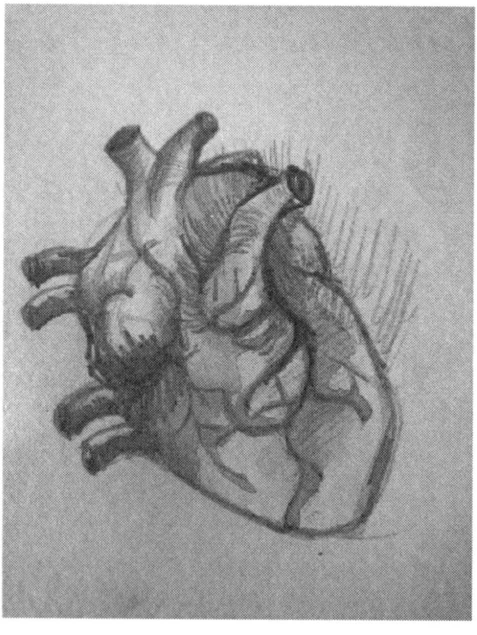

76 mosaic: (n) pieces of colored glass that creates an image; many found in the cathedrals of Constantinople

77 perne in a gyre: a spinning wheel image where the wheel spins both sides of a paper to create an image of movement

IV

Once out of nature I shall never take
My bodily form from any natural thing,
But such a form as Grecian[78] goldsmiths make
Of hammered gold and gold enameling
To keep a drowsy Emperor awake;
Or set upon a golden bough to sing
To lords and ladies of Byzantium
Of what is past, or passing, or to come.

78 Grecian: Greek

"Sailing to Byzantium" is the most inspired poem Yeats has ever written while also being considered one of the greatest poems of the 20th century. Written in 1926 when Yeats was 61, the poem addresses the anguish of old age. He refers to the aging body as a "tattered coat upon a stick." The narrator contemplates the creative work needed for the spirit to survive being "fastened to a dying animal" (the body). His answer is to leave the country of the young, sail "the seas and come / To the holy city of Byzantium," a place where sages can become "singing-masters" of his soul. While there, the sages can free his soul from his aging body, and like a great work of art, he could exist in the "artifice of eternity." Through the grace of art and beauty, he can be free from old age and never take his "bodily form from any natural thing." Instead, he could choose a more elemental form like golden clockwork bird, singing of the past, present, and future. The artificial world of art, which is timeless, is a way to free his energetic mind from his degrading natural body. Only through the active pursuit of the Arts is he truly free.

We should not take this poem as an actual journey, but as an imaginative one. To understand the poem more, we need to understand symbolism. Where all words have various meanings that can vary from person to person, their symbols are universally acknowledged. Red can mean passion, heat, and anger. However, color an octagon red and place it at an intersection in the road, and we know that it means "stop." That is the power of a symbol. Put a dove on a flag, and we know it means peace. What is somewhat troublesome is the fact that some symbols can have both positive and negative meanings.

Let's take the color red again. It can symbolize sin or guilt. Just look at the symbolism of the scarlet letter, an "A" set in red, and the stigma it gives Hester Prynne in Nathanial Hawthorne's *Scarlet Letter*. Caught in adultery, Hester had to wear the red badge as a symbol of her sin and dishonor. Now take the same color and place it on a national flag, and suddenly the symbols change from dishonor and guilt to sacrifice and courage. So, how do we know what the speaker means? How do we know if the speaker is being literal or symbolic? And if the speaker is being symbolic, which interpretation is the best? Often, the reader must use context, how the symbol is being used. However, the fact that there are no easy answers to these questions shows the richness that poetry offers. The more we read, the easier it is to understand symbolism and interpret it more accurately.

Reading poetry forces us to think about familiar experiences from a different perspective. **Theme**, which deals with the overall meaning, or the central idea, of a poem, is an element of poetry we should be aware of to understand the overall meaning. A poetic theme deals with an abstraction (such as war) that materializes through how a person, action, or image is represented in the poem (war is destructive through loss of innocence and life).

Do not think of a theme as merely a topic or action. A theme is more than a simple subject, like love, war, or religion; a theme is both a subject and a predicate. Thus, the theme of Yeats's Sailing to Byzantium is not just about old age, which is merely a topic of a poem, but life and vitality give way to death that only art can overcome. This more specific theme explicitly turns the abstract concept into a deeper meaning.

Theme also deals with concepts. For example, what draws you to a particular poem? To answer that question is to address the theme. Does the poem make you think? Offer you a new perspective? Help you create any new ideas on a subject? Whatever the poem does, it creates a moment in time to ponder certain issues or remember the ideals of the past. Just try reading a poem with distractions around you, and you will soon realize that it is hard to understand. Find a nice quiet place to read, and then let the ideas flow through you. Soon the poem starts to make sense, not only on a thematic level, but also on a personal level.

Another theme "Sailing to Byzantium" raises is that of an afterlife. The last stanza of the poem mentions the artificial golden bird "set upon a golden bough to sing." The golden bough is in reference to the story of Aeneas and the Golden Bough. Aeneas enters the underworld to visit the spirit of his departed father. Before he can enter, he must find a golden branch and offer it as a gift to the queen of the underworld. He finds his father resting in Elysium, a paradise for the souls of the just. Just as in this myth, "Sailing to Byzantium" deals with an eternal afterlife. Where Aeneas's Golden Bough is an offering to enter the afterlife without tasting death, Yeats's golden bough is where the narrator may dwell eternally in any pleasing form. His is an offering of knowledge "of what is past, or passing, or to come" (past, present, and future), a pure form of gold. Finally, father and son join into one blessed union in the myth. The father can show Aeneas his ancestors, the future of the Roman Empire, such as Romulus and Remus (the founders of Rome) and the Caesars (the rulers of the Golden Age of Rome). The narrator in Yeats's poem pursues his own vision of eternal life as well as the beginning of paradise, which is artistic rather than spiritual.

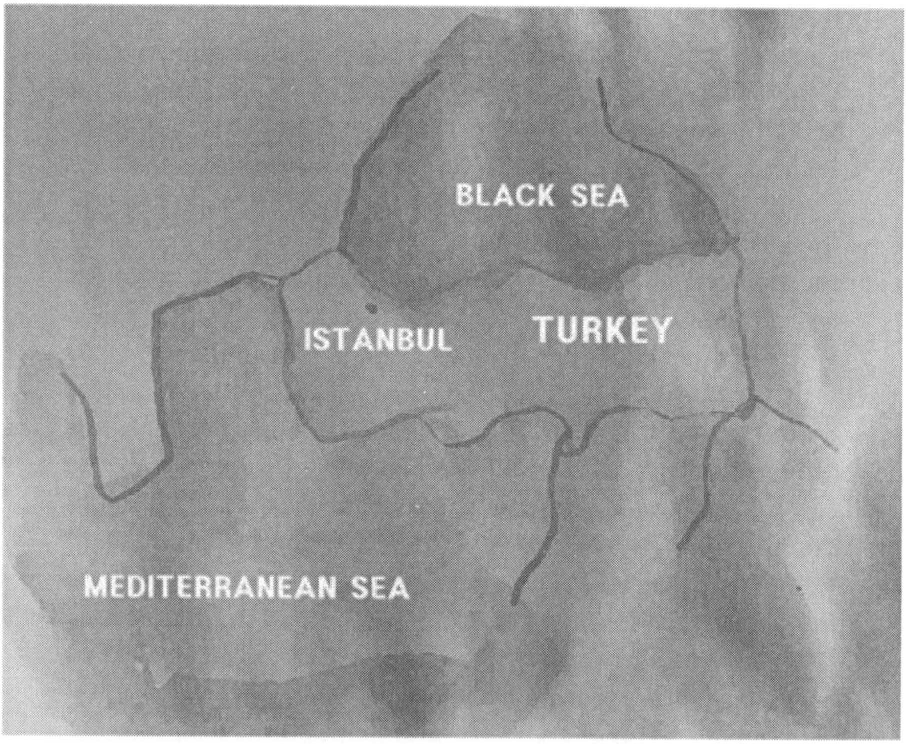
BLACK SEA
ISTANBUL
TURKEY
MEDITERRANEAN SEA

STOPPING BY THE WOODS ON A SNOWY EVENING

Robert Frost

Whose woods these are I think I know.
His house is in the village, though;
He will not see me stopping here
To watch his woods fill up with snow.

My little horse must think it queer
To stop without a farmhouse near
Between the woods and frozen lake
The darkest evening of the year.

He gives his harness bells a shake
To ask if there is some mistake.
The only other sound's the sweep

Of easy wind and downy flake.

The woods are lovely, dark, and deep,
But I have promises to keep,
And miles to go before I sleep,
And miles to go before I sleep.

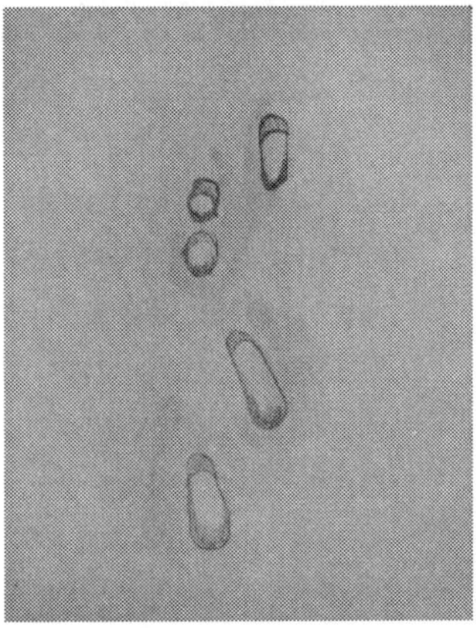

The theme of this poem can be solitude, but that would be missing the deeper meaning. More accurately, it can be stated that a solitary traveler contemplates his place in the wilderness. Almost every romantic poet writes of solitude, for to be a poet is to be on the outskirts of society. A poet is often on the fringes of the community, seen as an outcast, a strange oddity with a peculiar way with words. Being on the outside looking in allows the poet insight into the actual functions of society as well as the wonders of the natural world. The poet views the natural world with curiosity, anxiety, as well as respect. It is no coincidence, then, that Romantic poets romanticized the lone wanderer. We could say that the lonely wanderer in Frost's poem is even a **metaphor** of the poet's journey, and the horse he is riding is the reader.

The first stanza is like the poet viewing the natural world around him, wondering what it is exactly he is viewing. The second stanza is like the reader wondering about the strange choice of words chosen to convey such a thought. The reader may even "ask if there is some mistake." Nothing but the whiteness of the page responds back. The poem, indeed, is "lovely, dark and deep." But Frost does not linger too long on one poem; he does not overwrite, and his poetry is rather short, for he has other "promises to keep", or other poems to write. He has many more things to say before he can even sleep. The repetition of the last two lines gives a sense of weariness. The poet, like the rider, is tired, but must move one, must write, for there is a whole world to see or write of before the end of the journey. The journey may be long and lonely, but it will also be beautiful and wonderful.

Finally, notice the relationship between the horse and rider. The horse is domesticated and as such, follows the rules given to it. The poet feels comfortable on the fringe, this is his territory. The horse does not, and even questions why they are there (at least in the poet's mind). Just as the reader may question the sanity of the poet, it is ultimately the poet's duty to bring a sense of balance to a cold, dark world. This seems to be the poet's duty; what Frost saw as the poet's function in society.

A Brief Introduction to T.S. Eliot

(1888-1965)

Thomas Sterns Eliot is considered one of the most eminent literary figures of the 20th century, whose pre-war influences became his post-war ideology. Like Ezra Pound, Eliot was born in America but moved to England later in life and became a British citizen at the age of 39. He attended Harvard in 1906 to study philosophy and then furthered his studies in Germany and France. He settled in England when World War I started and continued his studies in Greek philosophy at Oxford University. He decided to stay in England to get married and work at a bank. In 1915, he started writing literary and philosophical reviews and published his first poem, "The Love Song of J. Alfred Prufrock" in a Chicago publication at the suggestion of Ezra Pound.

1922 was the year a publishing wonder changed literary thought of the 20th century: *The Wasteland*.

Critics praised Eliot's *The Wasteland* for its symbolism of the secluded individual created by a century of unbalance and beginning. It expressed in bold words the torment and emptiness found in a society after World War I. Unlike other major poets of the past, Eliot created and relied upon his own imagery to create his work instead of relying upon past ideas, which often makes reading his poetry difficult.

Eliot was originally of the Imagists, influenced by Hulme and Pound. Pound was instrumental in the formation of Eliot as the greatest poet of his time. Pound was also involved in editing and improving *The Wasteland*, cutting most of the traditional rhyming content (heroic couplets, and iambic pentameter). With Pound's urging, the many mini poems within this poem were also edited out, leaving a trimmer 434-line poem more fitting to the Imagist ideals. Eliot even dedicated the poem to his mentor, who was envious of the poem. Pound conceded that the student had outperformed the master. Once published, Eliot was able to move Imagism from the fringe of the literary world to the main literary culture of the century, something that Pound had been trying to do for fifteen years. Though Eliot strove to break away from the Victorian traditions by introducing myths, spiritual imagery, and allusion, he never met with critical success until 1922 when he was 44 years old.

Eliot also held to the philosophy of naturalism that most of his early poetry professed. Thus, his poetry was dark and internally bleak. A good example can be found in an excerpt from "The Winter Evening Settles Down." Eliot was the master of bringing images out of the Romantic era of beauty and nature to record what was experienced in the everyday dirt and grime of city streets.

The winter evening settles down
With smells of steaks in passageways.
Six o'clock.
The burnt-out ends of smoky days.
And now a gusty shower wraps
The grimy scraps
Of withered leaves across your feet
And newspapers from vacant lots;
The showers beat

On empty blinds and chimney-pots,
And at the corner of the street
A lonely cab-horse steams and stamps.

And then the lighting of the lamps.

The images of winter are creatively altered. Romantic and Victorian poets would have written refreshing images of winter peace and tranquility surrounded by a blanket of crystal white snow in a rural setting. Eliot infuses naturalism and Imagism of a winter scene in the cold, dirty reality of city streets. Winter in London is far from enjoyable; it is often cold and bitter. Add a winter rain, and it becomes miserable. Eliot wonderfully describes concrete images of burnt-out cigarettes, grimy garbage, withered leaves, and empty blinds and chimney pots to conjure a world of sterility and destruction. He uses most of his five senses: the smell of steaks cooking; the feel of grimy scraps of withered leaves; the sound of rain beating on windows and chimneys; the sight of someone lighting the city lamps. These are called **concrete images**, for they stimulate senses directly as if the reader were there to witness the scene.

Two major events occurred after 1927. Eliot became a permanent English citizen, and he converted to the Anglican Church. Before his conversion, he grew up in a Unitarian household, and his grandfather founded the St. Louis Unitarian Church. This rigid unemotional type of religion did not sit well with Eliot, and in his school days he rejected Unitarianism. With his conversion to the more appealing and classical oriented Anglo-Catholicism in 1927, Eliot's poetry became lighter and more hopeful with the publication of "Ash Wednesday" (1930) and the "Four Quartets" (1935-1942). He managed to show his lighter, moralistic style without being dismissed as merely a religious poet. 1n 1948, he was awarded the Nobel Prize for literature.

THE LOVE SONG OF J. ALFRED PRUFROCK

T.S. Eliot

S'io credesse che mia risposta fosse
A persona che mai tornasse al mondo,
Questa fiamma staria senza piu scosse.
Ma perciocche giammai di questo fondo
Non torno vivo alcun, s'i'odo il vero,
Senza tema d'infamia ti rispondo[79].

Let us go then, you and I,
When the evening is spread out against the sky
Like a patient etherized[80] upon a table;

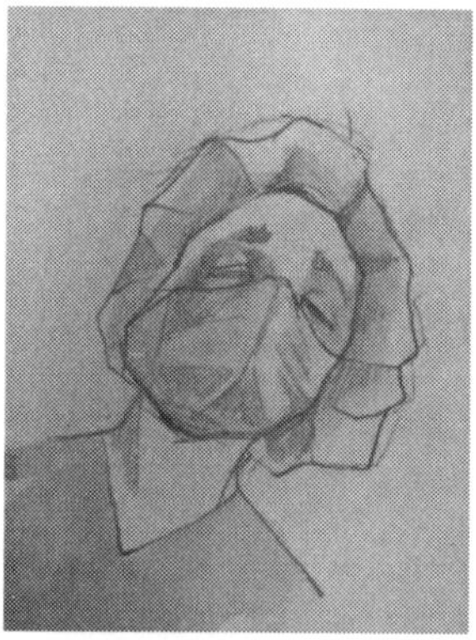

79 The following is translated from the original Italian as found in Dante's Inferno XXVII, 61-66:
If I thought my answer were given
To anyone who would ever return to the world,
This flame would stand still without moving any further.
But since never from this abyss
Has anyone ever returned alive, if what I hear is true,
Without fear of infamy I answer you.

80 etherized: (v) to be put under anesthesia

Let us go, through certain half-deserted streets,
The muttering retreats
Of restless nights in one-night cheap hotels
And sawdust restaurants with oyster-shells:

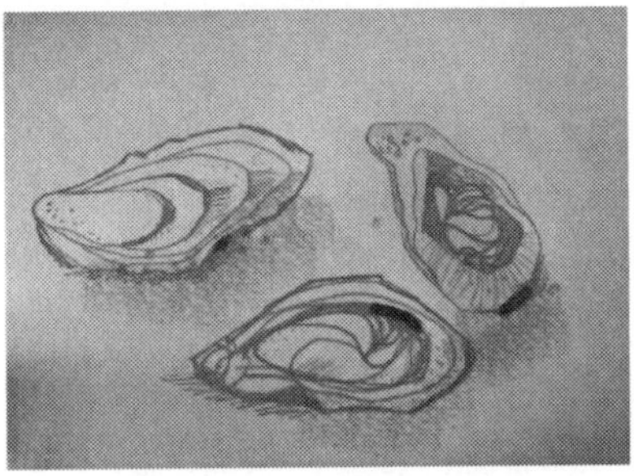

Streets that follow like a tedious argument
Of insidious intent
To lead you to an overwhelming question...
Oh, do not ask, "What is it?"
Let us go and make our visit.

In the room the women come and go
Talking of Michelangelo[81].

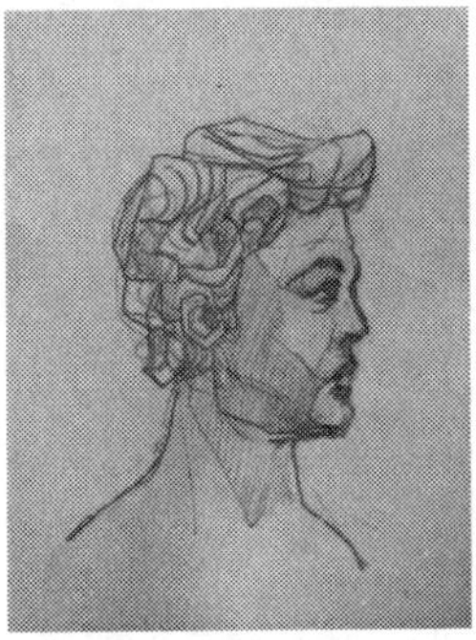

81 Michelangelo: (1475–1564) Italian artist

The yellow fog that rubs its back upon the window-panes,
The yellow smoke that rubs its muzzle[82] on the window-panes
Licked its tongue into the corners of the evening,

Lingered upon the pools that stand in drains,
Let fall upon its back the soot that falls from chimneys,
Slipped by the terrace, made a sudden leap,
And seeing that it was a soft October night,
Curled once about the house, and fell asleep.

And indeed there will be time
For the yellow smoke that slides along the street,
Rubbing its back upon the window-panes;
There will be time, there will be time
To prepare a face to meet the faces that you meet;
There will be time to murder and create,
And time for all the works and days of hands
That lift and drop a question on your plate;
Time for you and time for me,
And time yet for a hundred indecisions,
And for a hundred visions and revisions,

82 muzzle: (n) the jaws, mouth, and nose that extends from an animal's face. The fog is being personified

Before the taking of a toast and tea.

In the room the women come and go
Talking of Michelangelo.

And indeed there will be time
To wonder, "Do I dare?" and, "Do I dare?"
Time to turn back and descend the stair,
With a bald spot in the middle of my hair—
[They will say: "How his hair is growing thin!"]
My morning coat, my collar mounting firmly to the chin,
My necktie rich and modest, but asserted by a simple pin—
[They will say: "But how his arms and legs are thin!"]

Do I dare
Disturb the universe?
In a minute there is time
For decisions and revisions which a minute will reverse.

For I have known them all already, known them all—
Have known the evenings, mornings, afternoons,
I have measured out my life with coffee spoons;
I know the voices dying with a dying fall
Beneath the music from a farther room.
        So how should I presume?

And I have known the eyes already, known them all—
The eyes that fix you in a formulated phrase,
And when I am formulated, sprawling on a pin,
When I am pinned and wriggling on the wall,
Then how should I begin
To spit out all the butt-ends of my days and ways?
        And how should I presume?

And I have known the arms already, known them all—
Arms that are braceleted and white and bare
[But in the lamplight, downed with light brown hair!]
Is it perfume from a dress
That makes me so digress?
Arms that lie along a table, or wrap about a shawl.
        And should I then presume?
        And how should I begin?

. . .

Shall I say, I have gone at dusk through narrow streets
And watched the smoke that rises from the pipes
Of lonely men in shirt-sleeves, leaning out of windows?

...
I should have been a pair of ragged claws
Scuttling across the floors of silent seas.
...
And the afternoon, the evening, sleeps so peacefully!
Smoothed by long fingers,
Asleep... tired... or it malingers[83],
Stretched on the floor, here beside you and me.
Should I, after tea and cakes and ices,
Have the strength to force the moment to its crisis?
But though I have wept and fasted, wept and prayed,
Though I have seen my head [grown slightly bald] brought in upon a platter,
I am no prophet[84]—and here's no great matter;
I have seen the moment of my greatness flicker,
And I have seen the eternal Footman hold my coat, and snicker,
And in short, I was afraid.

83 malinger: (v) to pretend sickness to avoid a duty

84 Though I have seen my head...I am no prophet: refers to the prophet John the Baptist, beheaded by Herod and had his head offered upon a platter to Salome

And would it have been worth it, after all,
After the cups, the marmalade, the tea,
Among the porcelain, among some talk of you and me, to pretend sickness, esp. in order to shirk one's duty, avoid work
Would it have been worth while,
To have bitten off the matter with a smile,
To have squeezed the universe into a ball[85]
To roll it toward some overwhelming question,
To say: "I am Lazarus,[86] come from the dead,
Come back to tell you all, I shall tell you all"—
If one, settling a pillow by her head,
Should say: "That is not what I meant at all.
That is not it, at all."

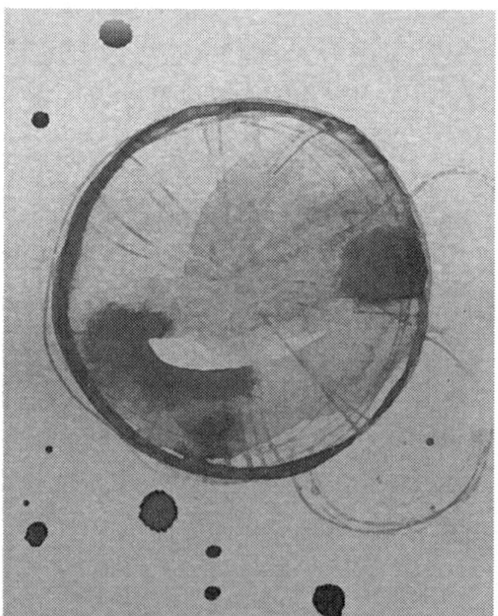

85 ...into a ball: a reference to the ball in Andrew Marvell's "To His Coy Mistress"

86 Lazarus: a man Jesus miraculously raised from the dead

And would it have been worth it, after all,
Would it have been worth while,
After the sunsets and the dooryards and the sprinkled streets,
After the novels, after the teacups, after the skirts that trail along the floor—
And this, and so much more?—
It is impossible to say just what I mean!
But as if a magic lantern threw the nerves in patterns on a screen:
Would it have been worth while
If one, settling a pillow or throwing off a shawl,
And turning toward the window, should say:
"That is not it at all,
That is not what I meant, at all."

. . . . .

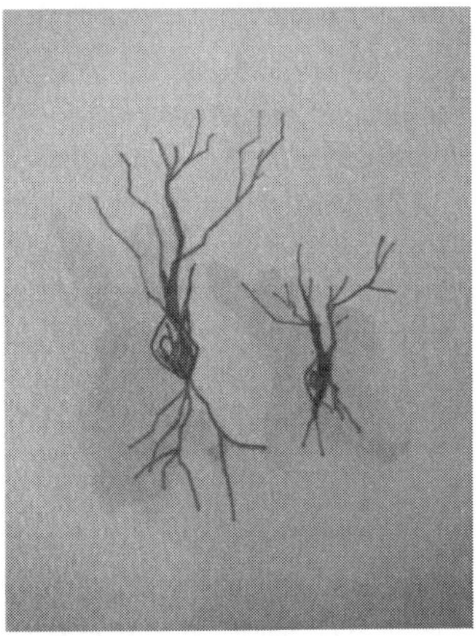

No! I am not Prince Hamlet[87], nor was meant to be;
Am an attendant lord, one that will do
To swell a progress, start a scene or two,
Advise the prince; no doubt, an easy tool,
Deferential[88], glad to be of use,
Politic, cautious, and meticulous;
Full of high sentence, but a bit obtuse[89];
At times, indeed, almost ridiculous—
Almost, at times, the Fool.

I grow old… I grow old…
I shall wear the bottoms of my trousers rolled.

Shall I part my hair behind? Do I dare to eat a peach?
I shall wear white flannel trousers, and walk upon the beach.
I have heard the mermaids singing, each to each.

I do not think that they will sing to me.
I have seen them riding seaward on the waves
Combing the white hair of the waves blown back
When the wind blows the water white and black.

We have lingered in the chambers of the sea
By sea-girls wreathed with seaweed red and brown
Till human voices wake us, and we drown.

87 Hamlet: a fictional prince of Denmark in Shakespeare's play who deals with madness over the death of his father and seeks to avenge his death only to cause the deaths of his close friends and loved ones.

88 deferential: (adj) respectful

89 obtuse: (adj) slow in thought

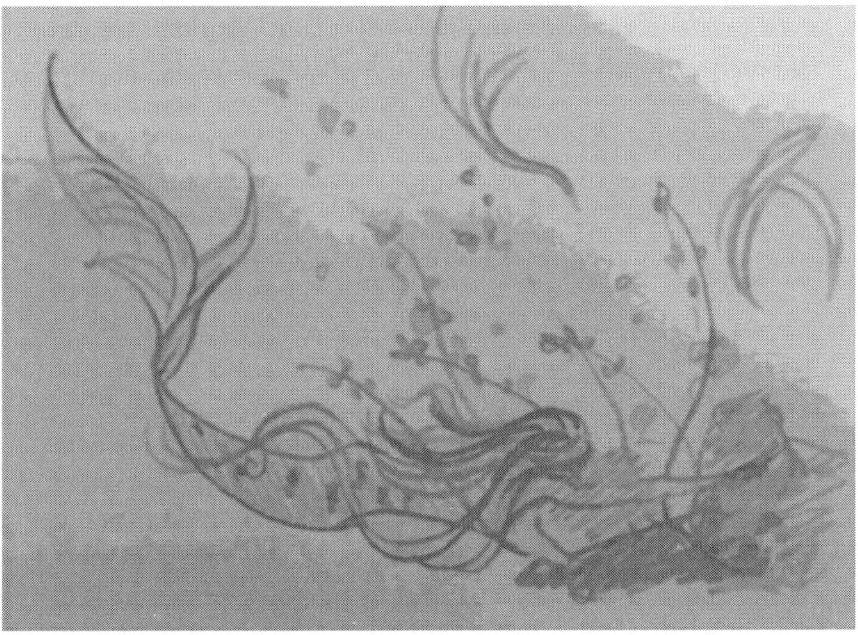

Eliot was also a formidable literary critic, influencing the thought of his time. He formulated the concept of **objective correlative** in his collection of essays *The Sacred Wood* (1920). This is the arousing of the reader's emotions through a pattern of objects, actions, or events without relying on a "formula" of those responses. His poem "The Love Song of J. Alfred Prufrock" is a perfect example of objective correlative. He mentions that in modern life human existence is often wasted and boring. Workers set out for the boredoms of their day through mundane rituals that have no purpose. "For I have known them all already, known them all: / Have known the evenings, mornings, afternoons, / I have measured out my life with coffee spoons."

Eliot was a classicist as well as a modern poet. He filled his poetry with classic images and forms, while paving the way for a new type of poetry that had never been written before. The most telling of this marriage of classicism and modernism is the title. As you read the title, you may find it odd. J. Alfred Prufrock is a rather modern name, and a stuffy one at that, yet he is the protagonist of a love poem. It sets up a theme that is dominant is most of Eliot's earlier poetry: the difference between classical romance and realism.

The poem offers an epigram with a classical quote in the original Italian from Dante's *Inferno* (14th century). In the **epic**, Dante meets a miserable soul in the underworld, who is so desperate for companionship, he tells Dante his tale. The sinner offers this information since he thinks Dante will never return to the world of the living to spread his infamy. This small quote offered by Eliot establishes the overall theme: the loneliness and isolation of a man unable to tell his story, which is exactly the problem Prufrock is having at the start of the poem.

The poem starts with Prufrock speaking to someone, "Let us go, you and I, / When the evening is spread out against the sky." This is probably Prufrock's romantic self talking to his realist self as he wishes for a relationship that will end his loneliness. The only problem is he feels "like a patient etherized upon a table." What a shocking image for the start of a love poem. However, it does establish Prufrock's paralysis in the face of meeting others. It also conjures images of dissection, which are scattered throughout the poem to remind us of the agony he feels, for he will be taken apart psychologically by the poem's end. We get images of hands, eyes, arms, and long fingers. Then he references the beheading of John the Baptist, "Though I have seen my head [grown slightly bald] brought in upon a platter, I am no prophet—and here's no great matter."

The stanza then ends with the reason Prufrock is wandering these dark and dirty streets. He is going to visit someone at a party where "women come and go / Talking of Michelangelo." These two lines indicate that to many, the past is preferable to the present. As the women talk of the Renaissance genius Michelangelo, how is Prufrock supposed to insert himself into the conversation. Thus, he just argues with himself to speak with some woman. "To wonder, 'Do I dare?' and, 'Do I dare?' / Time to turn back and descend the stair, / With a bald spot in the middle of my hair." He dares not—so much for the love song—for he feels inferior to such great men of the past. Other larger-than-life men are brought up throughout the poem, adding to this inferiority complex: Hamlet, John the Baptist, and Lazarus risen from the dead.

Thus, the reason for Prufrock's inhibitions is revealed. He is balding, short, and skinny. He feels he has no physical attractiveness to women. He does not fit the "heroic" male mold of classical romance. If only he knew that his romantic mind and sensibility is enough to attract most women. Then Prufrock gives some wonderful realistic images. He ceaselessly passes his days one cup of coffee at a time, like sand through an hour glass while others observe him as an inferior male "sprawling on a pin, / When I am pinned and wriggling on the wall." This is a rather poignant observation of his own failed nerves to speak with the woman at the party. "How should I begin?"

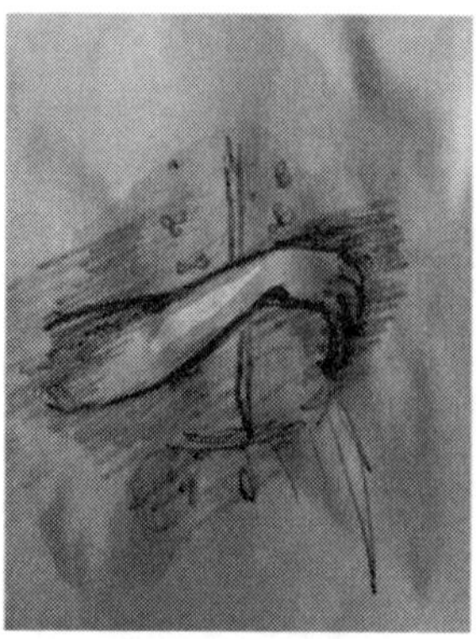

The romantic self answers with an idealistic description of a lady's arms. "Arms that are braceleted and white and bare." The realistic self then butts in and says, "[But in the lamplight, downed with light brown hair!]" He sees other's faults and failings too clearly, even his own, to be

romantic. So, how should he begin to address the woman? Should he tell her he is lonely and seen his own future? "Watched the smoke that rises from the pipes / Of lonely men in shirt-sleeves, leaning out of windows?" No. He simply gives up and feels reduced to a simple solitary animal, "I should have been a pair of ragged claws / Scuttling across the floors of silent seas." This form would be so much better than a complex human overwhelmed by emotions. He is human, however, and continues his rationalizing and suffering.

Prufrock spends the rest of his afternoons and evenings lazing around and sleeping, alone with his thoughts and his own arguments with himself. Again, he bemoans his inferiority complex. If only he were great enough to be beheaded as John the Baptist. Except, if he were, he would have that terrible bald spot that everyone would notice. Then he recalls when he has entered houses and given his coat to the footmen, who only snickered at his deteriorating looks. He then falls into melancholy and asks a series of rhetorical questions. Would all the fuss that goes into a dating a woman be worthwhile? What if he did all that is required, and she lay on a pillow next him only to reject him because he had misspoken or acted inappropriately. "That's not what I meant at all." In his mind, he has already failed before he even starts. So much for the love song.

In the end, Prufrock compares himself to Hamlet. Not that he thinks himself princely, but because he delays before he takes any action. It takes the whole play for Hamlet to avenge the death of his father after much contemplation. Even that comparison is too generous, he thinks, so he likens himself to Hamlet's advisor Polonius, "an easy tool, deferential." So, what does he advise himself?

Well, both the realist Prufrock and the romantic one answer. The realist says, "grow old... I grow old." Whereupon the romantic replies, "I will wear the bottoms of my trousers rolled," which was becoming fashionable in his day. The realist them comments, "I shall wear white flannel trousers and walk upon the beach." He is to be alone. The romantic self urges him to view the mermaids singing to each other; he can find comfort in a world of fantasy. Whereas, the realist retorts, "I do not think that they will sing to me."

The romantic Prufrock gives hope one last try. "I have seen them riding seaward on the waves / Combing the white hair of the waves blown back / When the wind blows the water white and black." However, Prufrock is a modern man. He is not suited for either the world of the past nor for the world of the present. He is lost. Almost content in the world of fantasy he has created, Prufrock is woken by human voices and drowned. In other words, he ends his "song" in the same state he started it, etherized on a table, dissected like an insect, and still very much alone.

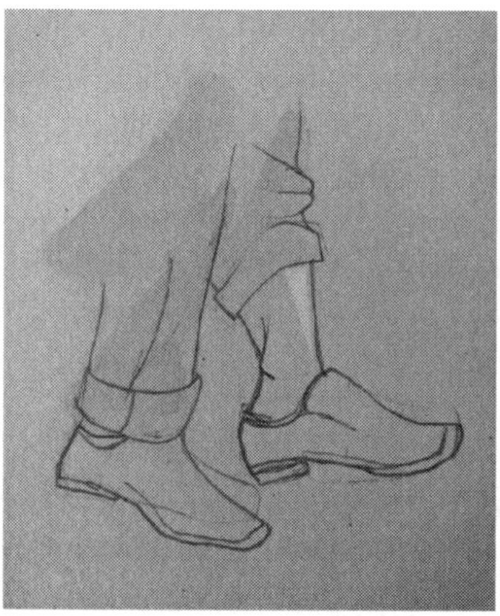

THEME FOUR: FREEDOM

Freedom has various contexts, but we will look at how our featured poets view freedom as both an internal and external desire. As far as having internal freedom, many would think of self-reliance, others would equate spiritual freedom as well, including inner peace, self-control, and a sense of free will. With external freedom, ideas of not being dominated by another or having a government that upholds general liberties usually come to mind. Rebellion and revolution are cries for freedom from a suppressed state. Freedom is often equated with happiness, and it parallels with religion because religious freedom often leads to freedom of the soul from the bondage of sin or guilt.

William Blake championed external freedom in what he saw as a bleak, dark age. As one of the forerunners of the Romantic Period, Blake was concerned with the abolishment of slaves, the rights of women, and the abuse of the poor by the wealthy.

LONDON

William Blake

I wander through each chartered street,
Near where the chartered Thames does flow,
And mark in every face I meet
Marks of weakness, marks of woe.

In every cry of every man,
In every infant's cry of fear,
In every voice, in every ban,
The mind-forged manacles I hear:

How the chimney-sweeper's cry
Every black'ning church appalls;
And the hapless soldier's sigh
Runs in blood down Palace walls.

But most, through midnight streets I hear
How the youthful harlot's curse
Blasts the new-born Infant's tear,
And blights with plagues the Marriage-hearse.

In "London," Blake concentrates on the problems of personal freedom and social justice in the London of his time. In sharp contrast to the pastoral images in his "Songs of Innocence," Blake opens his poem with the image of every street and even the mighty river Thames being chartered, being partitioned to ownership by some lord or owner. Nothing in London is free or natural. On top of that, we have restricting laws, a religion that is no longer pure ("black'ning church appalls"), excessive poverty, and starving children that lead to more crime and suffering such as disease and prostitution. Notice that none of the people he talks about are seen; they are only heard through their sighs or cries or have left traces of blood. This is the world of experience for Blake and any talk of freedom is but a laughable expression as long as religious authorities and the upper class turn a blind eye to the situation.

A Brief Introduction to Lord George Gordon Byron

(1788-1824)

Just as William Blake may seem like an odd fit for Romanticism, so does Lord Byron. However, he continues to be the ultimate example of Romantic poetry. He considered his contemporaries to be on the wrong path with their poetry, and that it contained little substance. By the age of nineteen, Byron had started publishing poetry in lyrical verse. He published a small volume called *Hours of Idleness* (1807). The critics were not favorable to it at first, and such scathing reviews caused Byron to attack his critics back. He responded with the satirical poem "English Bards and Scotch Reviewers" (1809), which attacked not only his critics but also the poetry of all his contemporaries, including Wordsworth and Coleridge. His greatest work "Don Juan" (1819-1824) returned to the neoclassic ideals and satire of Pope and Swift. However, Byron labeled himself as the "arch-romantic." Though his work is clearly romantic in tone, his mood and desire to be apart from the mainstream romantic poets was well known, for Lord Byron is truly in a class of his own.

Perhaps the best-known device of his poetry is the **Byronic Hero**, found mostly in "Manfred" (1817), "Childe Harold" (1812-1818), "The Prisoner of Chillon" (1816), and "Don Juan." The Byronic Hero often rebels and then suffers exile, while his talent and passions help bring about self-destruction. An isolated, defiant, and dark character, the Byronic Hero became closely associated with Byron himself. Many of his readers thought these poems were somewhat autobiographical, which was not the case. Perhaps the Byronic Hero is such that the art eventually shaped the man. What Byron had in common with his heroes was a suppressed guilt that compelled both him and them to an unavoidable end.

Byron's lifestyle and writing inspired a new generation of guilt-ridden Byronic heroes in literature, such as Captain Ahab in *Moby Dick*. Byron was often considered a womanizer, though women often pursued him. Byron married Anne Isabella Milbanke in 1815, more out of the need to avoid women. A year later, they separated when he had an incestuous affair with his half-sister Augusta Leigh, whom he never met until adulthood. The affair with Augusta did not please the powers of England, and in 1816, they banished him from England. He settled in Geneva and started a close companionship with the poet Percy Bysshe Shelley. Byron ended up having a child with Shelley' s sister-in-law, 17-year-old Claire Clairmont. He moved to Venice in 1817, where he finished "Childe Harold." Seeking sanctuary from his life of debauchery, Byron moved to Pisa, Italy, where he met up with Shelley again and started another close literary circle but suffered more criticism of his poetry.

Perhaps out of guilt, and the need to better himself as a human being, Byron moved to Greece to assist the Greeks in their war for independence from the Ottoman Empire. Using his fame and notoriety throughout Europe, Byron created sympathy for the Greek cause. He used his own funds to arm Greek soldiers under him and, though he wasn't a soldier, would fight with them. He lived in dismal conditions, knowing his cause was just. Unfortunately, he grew sick before he could leave and succumbed to feverish attacks. At the age of thirty-six, Lord George Gordon Byron, the sixth Baron, died fighting for what he believed in.

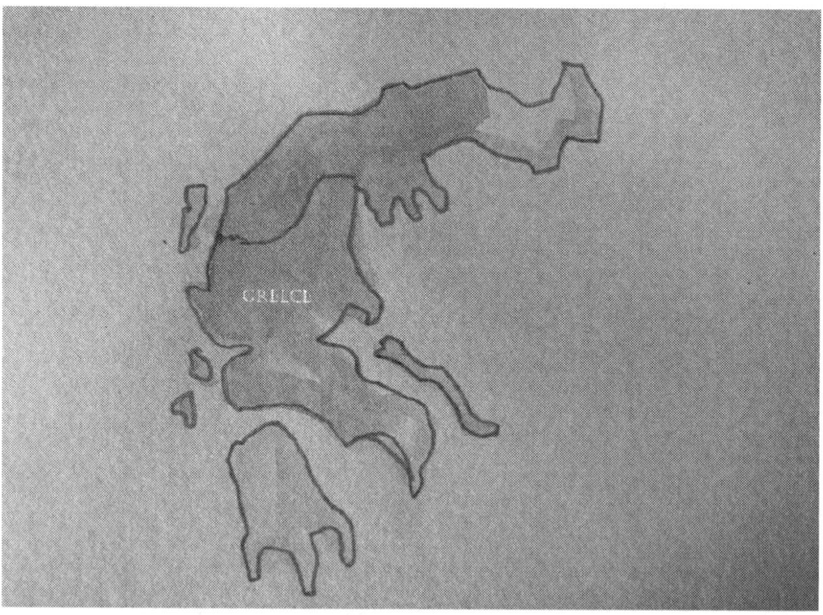

SONNET ON CHILLON[90]

Lord George G. Byron

Eternal spirit of the chainless mind!
Brightest in dungeons, Liberty! thou art,
For there thy habitation is the heart,
The heart which love of thee alone can bind;

And when thy sons to fetters[91] are consigned[92]
To fetters, and the damp vault's dayless gloom,
Their country conquers with their martyrdom,
And Freedom's fame finds wings on every wind.

Chillon! thy prison is a holy place,
And thy sad floor an altar, for 'twas trod,
Until his very steps have left a trace

90 Chillon: a castle located on the shore of Lake Geneva, Switzerland that once held Francois Bonnivard

91 fetter: (n) a chain fastened to the feet

92 consign: (v) to give over the care of one person or thing to another

Worn, as if thy cold pavement were a sod,
By Bonnivard![93] - May none those marks efface![94]
For they appeal from tyranny to God.

93 Bonnivard: Francois Bonnivard (1496-1570), the Genovois monk imprisoned in Chillon from 1532 to 1536. At a young age, Francois opposed Charles III, the Duke of Savoy, from taking control of Geneva. For his rebellious efforts, Bonnivard was imprisoned in Chillon for three years.

94 efface: (v) to erase

Lord Byron had great disdain for social institutions that refused to reform or allow personal freedoms to all classes. However, his works captured his spirit to such a degree that most of his characters bear his name as Byronic heroes. Such heroes show dislike for social institutions and accompanying rank and privileges. They often rebel and then suffer exile, while their great talent and passion help to bring about self-destruction.

Though it is but a sonnet, "The Sonnet of Chillon" features an actual person that is an ideal **Byronic hero**; thus, this character's life drew Byron to his story like a magnet. Chillon is a castle on the shore of Lake Geneva in Switzerland that once held a Genovois monk, Francois Bonnivard, from 1532 to 1536. At a young age, Francois opposed Charles III, the Duke of Savoy, from taking control of Geneva. For his rebellious efforts, Bonnivard was imprisoned for three years. Upon his release, he continued his rebellion. He was imprisoned yet again for six years in Chillon, "brightest of dungeons." He was freed after the fall of the Duke. Obviously, Byron felt such characters who upheld others' freedoms over their own were worthy of praise.

A Brief Introduction to Percy Bysshe Shelley

(1792-1822)

No other major poet has ever gone through as much critical doubt as Percy Shelley. He was very much an outcast all his life. Though other poets like Wordsworth, Byron, and W.B. Yeats praised his artistic style, he was never understood or fully appreciated. Born of an aristocratic family, he always had the means and the money to become a literary giant. Never to rest upon what was done before him, he used his great talent to speak out against the moral decline of society. Though he was in line to receive a Baron title and given the education for it, Shelley shocked his family and Oxford when he published *The Necessity of Atheism* (1810). Oxford expelled him because he failed to prove that God did not exist without any conclusive scientific evidence. All hopes of any career in academia were lost.

Shelley settled in London to find a niche to voice his philosophies and to express his revolutionary spirit. When he was eighteen, he eloped with Harriet Westbrook. Since she was only sixteen, this caused a scandal with both families. They were forced to move around to find work to support their two children. In 1813, Shelley returned to London and published his first major poem, "Queen Mab," which supported social and political reform and spoke out against established traditions like marriage and religion.

By 1814, Shelley, showing his contempt for the traditional institution of marriage, left Harriet for the new love of his life, Mary Wollstonecraft Godwin. Mary's father was a major influence on Shelley in his youth. Because of the immoral nature of their actions, Shelley and Mary left for France. Showing that he respected his ex-wife, though he no longer loved her, he invited Harriet to live with them.

This last act caused Shelley's parents to disown him.

When the Shelleys returned to London a year later, Shelley discovered he was detested, and all who knew him were disgusted with his immorality. To make matters worse, Harriet had several love affairs and became pregnant, so in 1816 she drowned herself. Losing the right to care for the child, Shelley married Mary and fled to Italy, scorned by his own countrymen. In Italy he wrote some great poetry. First, he penned "Mutability," a meditation upon life and death. Another was "To Wordsworth" (1816), a poem criticizing and grieving over Wordsworth's softening on his social radicalism. Shelley lost his health due to constant travel and never having a place to settle down. Two more children were born to him and died nine months later.

Feeling the dread of poverty, exile, death, and misunderstanding, Shelley wrote some of his best poetry in Italy. His first was a tragedy "The Cenci" (1820). He followed this up with his most celebrated poem; a lyrical drama entitled *Prometheus Unbound* (1820). His mature poetry is highly influenced by the writing of Plato and the Neo-Platonists. His lyrical poems of note are "Ode to the West Wind" and "Ozymandias" (1818), which is the Greek name for Ramses II of 13th century Egypt. Shelley was able to use allegory rather effectively in his poetry, and "Ozymandias" is a perfect example of this.

OZYMANDIAS

Percy Bysshe Shelley

I met a traveller from an antique land
Who said: "Two vast and trunkless legs of stone
Stand in the desert. Near them on the sand,
Half sunk, a shattered visage lies, whose frown
And wrinkled lip and sneer of cold command
Tell that its sculptor well those passions read
Which yet survive, stamped on these lifeless things,
The hand that mocked them and the heart that fed.
And on the pedestal these words appear:
'My name is Ozymandias, King of Kings:
Look on my works, ye[95] mighty, and despair!'
Nothing beside remains. Round the decay
Of that colossal wreck, boundless and bare,
The lone and level sands stretch far away".

95 ye: (prn) classical form of you

The symbols that Shelley plays with are of power and sovereignty, which are usually represented through both the deeds of mighty men and the monuments they leave behind. In the poem a traveler discovers the ruins of Ozymandias's giant statue. It is nothing more than a pile of stones with the inscription at its ruined feet, "My name is Ozymandias, king of kings: / Look on my works, ye Mighty, and despair!" However, the **irony** is that the statue is no longer mighty or frightening enough to cause despair. The only thing to despair is the fallen condition of this monument, which has nothing to do with the skill of a mighty pharaoh, but the craft of a lowly sculptor. Art exceeds ambition, as this poem also testifies.

In fact, another layer of allegory is that the statue and its symbolism must despair in the face of the mighty age of modernity. For Shelley, the idea of arrogance common with tyrannical leaders was almost laughable. The poem was written three years after Napoleon Bonaparte's crushing defeat at Waterloo and the demise of the French Empire; what started out as a revolution against tyranny that many in England supported, turned into tyranny and oppression again when Napoleon declared himself Emperor. Many, including Shelley, became disheartened by the hope that such a revolution could ever happen in England. In "Ozymandias," Shelley shows that the mighty pharaoh's own efforts to remain immortal throughout history are futile, and Napoleon'

s efforts, like Ozymandias's, will soon end as "a shattered visage." However, the **irony** of this allegory is not lost, for the name of Ozymandias still lives on as does the memory of his lost civilization, and though this poem is somewhat critical of the pharaoh's arrogance, Ramses continues to live on through the very lines of this poem.

Shelley was only thirty when he died. On July 8, 1822, Shelley and a friend took a sailing trip. Hitting a sudden storm, their boat sank, and their bodies washed ashore. The short time that Shelley wrote was not enough to establish him as a great poet of his time, a misfortune that could have been fixed if he had only time to mature and prove his writing excelled his lifestyle.

ODE TO THE WEST WIND

Percy Bysshe Shelley

I

O wild West Wind, thou breath of Autumn's being,
Thou, from whose unseen presence the leaves dead
Are driven, like ghosts from an enchanter fleeing,

Yellow, and black, and pale, and hectic red,
Pestilence-stricken multitudes: O thou,
Who chariotest [96]to their dark wintry bed

The wingèd seeds, where they lie cold and low,
Each like a corpse within its grave, until
Thine azure[97] sister of the Spring shall blow

Her clarion[98] o'er the dreaming earth, and fill
(Driving sweet buds like flocks to feed in air)
With living hues and odors plain and hill:

Wild Spirit, which art moving everywhere;
Destroyer and Preserver; hear, O hear!

---

96 chariotest: (v) to carry

97 azure: (adj) sky blue

98 clarion: (n) a curved trumpet

II

Thou on whose stream, 'mid the steep sky's commotion,
Loose clouds like Earth's decaying leaves are shed,
Shook from the tangled boughs of Heaven and Ocean,

Angels of rain and lightning: there are spread
On the blue surface of thine airy surge,
Like the bright hair uplifted from the head

Of some fierce Maenad,[99] even from the dim verge
Of the horizon to the zenith's height,
The locks of the approaching storm. Thou dirge

Of the dying year, to which this closing night
Will be the dome of a vast sepulcher
Vaulted with all thy congregated might

Of vapors, from whose solid atmosphere
Black rain, and fire, and hail will burst: O hear!

99 Maenad: the mad female worshippers of the Dionysus, the Greek god of wine and fertility

III

Thou who didst waken from his summer dreams
The blue Mediterranean, where he lay,
Lulled by the coil of his crystalline streams,

Beside a pumice[100] isle in Baiae's[101] bay,
And saw in sleep old palaces and towers
Quivering within the wave's intenser day,

All overgrown with azure moss and flowers
So sweet, the sense faints picturing them! Thou
For whose path the Atlantic's level powers

Cleave themselves into chasms, while far below
The sea-blooms and the oozy woods which wear
The sapless foliage of the ocean, know

Thy voice, and suddenly grow grey with fear,
And tremble and despoil themselves: O hear!

100 pumice: (n) a porous stone of volcanic glass

101 Baiae: an ancient resort city in SW Italy

IV

If I were a dead leaf thou mightest bear;
If I were a swift cloud to fly with thee;
A wave to pant beneath thy power, and share

The impulse of thy strength, only less free
Than thou, O Uncontrollable! If even
I were as in my boyhood, and could be

The comrade of thy wanderings over Heaven,
As then, when to outstrip thy skiey[102] speed
Scarce seemed a vision; I would ne'er have striven

As thus with thee in prayer in my sore need.
Oh! lift me as a wave, a leaf, a cloud!
I fall upon the thorns of life! I bleed!

A heavy weight of hours has chained and bowed
One too like thee: tameless, and swift, and proud.

102 skiey: (adj) of the sky

V

Make me thy lyre,[103] even as the forest is:
What if my leaves are falling like its own!
The tumult of thy mighty harmonies

Will take from both a deep, autumnal tone,
Sweet though in sadness. Be thou, Spirit fierce,
My spirit! Be thou me, impetuous[104] one!

Drive my dead thoughts over the universe
Like withered leaves to quicken a new birth!
And, by the incantation of this verse,

Scatter, as from an unextinguished hearth
Ashes and sparks, my words among mankind!
Be through my lips to unawakened Earth

The trumpet of a prophecy! O Wind,
If Winter comes, can Spring be far behind?

103 lyre: (n) a musical strumming instrument

104 impetuous: (adj) doing rash action

Shelley's "Ode to the West Wind" deals with internal freedom and the wish to move that freedom outward to bring change in others. Sections I through III deal with how the wind influences the earth, wind, and water. There is a sense of freedom in how Shelley alliteratively describes the "wild West Wind," and its ability to go anywhere and do as it pleases. Section IV deals with the narrator asking the wind for its power of movement since he, as an earthbound man, can hardly do what he wishes. Section V has the narrator asking the wind to be his own spirit, or muse as it were, and take his ideas of "dead thoughts" like dead leaves and spread them throughout the world. As a poet, the narrator feels free in thought and imagination but stuck upon the earth without any way of letting the world know his thoughts. The wind could serve as "The trumpet of a prophecy," to bring about a change in humanity. If the world is tired and dead in the wintry grip of tyrants and kings, perhaps with his words blowing through the wind, spring is not too far off.

Women Writers of the 19th Century

Though Plato viewed a republic where men and women were equal, women's citizenship had been ignored since Aristotle's exclusion of the female from the public realm. He considered women inferior in intellect, and because of this, they had no authority to reason at the same level of men in public affairs. Though women have managed to defeat this error in history, women's citizenship rights continue to be marginalized within historical studies even up through the 20th century. Most people can name Wordsworth, Coleridge, and Bryon as Romantic writers but fail to name any women writers. Thankfully, in the 21st century, study about women writers is finally starting to change. Many critics have found women's writing in the 1790's had created new criteria combining social, political, and economic meanings beyond literature.

In the late 18th and early 19th century, women were granted education but were not given any way to use their education. They were allowed to travel to broaden their horizons, so they could add to the prestige of their husbands and raise their children properly. Education was a tool for a woman to marry out of her social class, to rise and impress a man to marry, but once married she was to care for the children and attend to the servants. As the middle class started to grow, and competition for jobs increased, many men were taking lesser jobs, losing their jobs, or seeing their businesses fail. Thus, women had

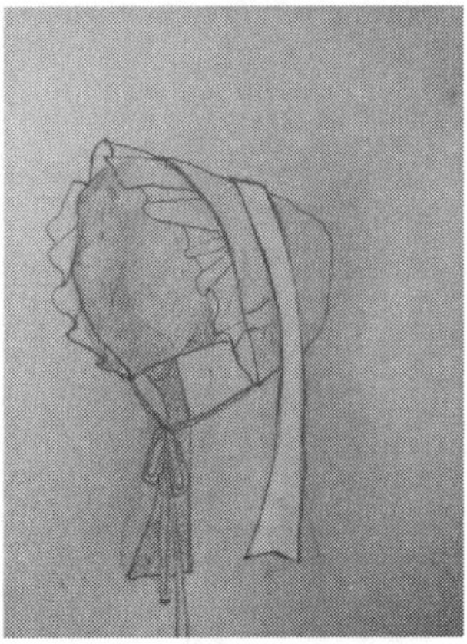

to find ways to make money. Having no opportunity to learn a skill, women had few options but to write. With their writing becoming popular enough that they could support their families, women were able to use their own names proudly instead of masculine pseudonyms. Unfortunately, the money they did make was not truly theirs. It belonged to their fathers or husbands.

Women were still excluded from literary circles, so they started to meet in their own. Since men were educated with higher learning that was denied women, women would study on their own, usually in the family library. Women would also learn Greek and Latin, so they could talk to other male writers. Soon the number of women writers started to grow beyond the men. Some scholars have found over 900 women listed as poets alone in the 19th century. They were successfully selling books and gaining literary reputations as poets, social commentators, and novelists.

As part of their popularity and success, women writers applied their own thoughts and feelings into what they knew best, domesticity and the plight of the poor and abused. Knowing what it was like to be outcast and treated as inferior, the women poets quickly picked up the plight

of those in slavery and advocated their freedom. Since they were writing against male conventions, female writers would often break those rules to create their own voice and tone. Many women saw children as another marginalized group. Thus, many pushed for more widespread reading among children of all classes, so they wrote many popular children's books and poems for the moral development of young minds.

A Brief Introduction to Anna Laetitia Barbauld

(1743-1825)

John Aikin Sr. had two notable children, John Aikin Jr. (1747-1822), another advocate of religious freedom, and Anna Laetitia (Aikin) Barbauld. Anna received an excellent education from her father and even learned how to read at the age of three. In 1771, her younger brother John encouraged her to write and publish poetry. She published six of her poems in his book, *Essays on Song-Writing*. By 1773, she published her own successful collection in *Poems*. Later poets such as Samuel Taylor Coleridge and William Wordsworth expressed their respect for her verse.

Marriage to Rochement Barbauld, a Unitarian minister, in 1774 showed in her writings as she mused over her love and friendship with her husband. Though they had no children of their own, they established a boarding school for boys and even adopted her brother's third son. Much of her poetry at this time reflected her experiences with children as found in the very religious *Hymns in Prose for Children* (1781). Being the most popular, it was translated into several European languages. She cowrote with her brother John another volume of poetry for children, *Evenings at Home* (1792).

By 1790, Anna's writing shifted toward the political turmoil of the time, and she used her prominence as a literary figure to speak out about the *Sins of the Government, Sins of the Nation* (1793). Like other female writers of her day, she favored abolition, championed the legislative power of the people, and supported religious liberty. All this caused her to be harshly criticized and rebuked. She published another volume of poems *Eighteen Hundred and Eleven* (1812) that heavily criticized England's war with France during the Napoleonic Wars, already into its tenth year. In this volume, she foretells the end of the British Empire. The criticism that followed was so harsh she would never publish again. However, several volumes of her poems were published posthumously by her niece, Lucy Aikin.

WASHING DAY

Anna Laetitia Barbauld

The Muses[105] are turned gossips; they have lost
The buskined[106] step, and clear high-sounding phrase,
Language of gods. Come, then, domestic Muse,
In slip-shod measure loosely prattling on,
Of farm or orchard, pleasant curds and cream,
Or droning flies, or shoes lost in the mire
By little whimpering boy, with rueful face —
Come, Muse, and sing the dreaded washing day.
Ye who beneath the yoke of wedlock bend,
With bowed soul, full well ye ken[107] the day
Which week, smooth sliding after week, brings on
Too soon; for to that day nor peace belongs,
Nor comfort; ere the first grey streak of dawn,
The red-armed washers come and chase repose.
Nor pleasant smile, nor quaint device of mirth,
Ere visited that day; the very cat,
From the wet kitchen scared, and reeking hearth,
Visits the parlor, an unwonted guest.
The silent breakfast meal is soon dispatched,
Uninterrupted, save by anxious looks
Cast at the louring, if sky should lour[108].
From that last evil, oh preserve us, heavens!

105 Muses: the goddesses of inspiration. Poets would often invoke their aid before attempting to write an epic.

106 buskined: (adj) tragic

107 ken: (v) archaic form meaning recognize

108 lour: (v) lower

For should the skies pour down, adieu to all
Remains of quiet; then expect to hear
Of sad disasters — dirt and gravel stains
Hard to efface, and loaded lines at once
Snapped short, and linen-horse by dog thrown down,
And all the petty miseries of life.
Saints have been calm while stretched upon the rack,
And Montezuma[109] smiled on burning coals;
But never yet did housewife notable
Greet with a smile a rainy washing day.
But grant the welkin[110] fair, require not thou
Who callest thyself, perchance, the master there,

109 Montezuma: Moctezuma II, the ruler of Meso America from 1466-1520, conquered by Cortez. Upon his death, Montezuma was cremated.

110 welkin: (n) the sky above.

Or study swept, or nicely dusted coat,
Or usual 'tendence; ask not, indiscreet,
Thy stockings mended, though the yawning rents
Gape wide as Erebus[111]; nor hope to find
Some snug recess impervious. Shouldst thou try
The 'customed garden walks, thine eye shall rue
The budding fragrance of thy tender shrubs,
Myrtle or rose, all crushed beneath the weight
Of coarse-checked apron, with impatient hand

Twitched off when showers impend; or crossing lines
Shall mar thy musings, as the wet cold sheet
Flaps in thy face abrupt. Woe to the friend
Whose evil stars have urged him forth to claim

111 Erebus: the underworld. Here referencing a gaping hole in the sock the size of the underworld

On such a day the hospitable rites;
Looks blank at best, and stinted courtesy
Shall he receive; vainly he feeds his hopes
With dinner of roast chicken, savory pie,
Or tart or pudding; pudding he nor tart
That day shall eat; nor, though the husband try —
Mending what can't be helped — to kindle mirth
From cheer deficient, shall his consort's brow
Clear up propitious; the unlucky guest
In silence dines, and early slinks away.
I well remember, when a child, the awe
This day struck into me; for then the maids,
I scarce knew why, looked cross, and drove me from them;
Nor soft caress could I obtain, nor hope
Usual indulgencies; jelly or creams,
Relic of costly suppers, and set by
For me their petted one; or buttered toast,
When butter was forbid; or thrilling tale
Of ghost, or witch, or murder. So I went
And sheltered me beside the parlour fire;
There my dear grandmother, eldest of forms,
Tended the little ones, and watched from harm;
Anxiously fond, though oft her spectacles
With elfin cunning hid, and oft the pins
Drawn from her ravelled stocking, might have soured
One less indulgent.
At intervals my mother's voice was heard,
Urging dispatch; briskly the work went on,
All hands employed to wash, to rinse, to wring,
Or fold, and starch, and clap[112], and iron, and plait.
Then would I sit me down, and ponder much

112 clap: (v) to flatten

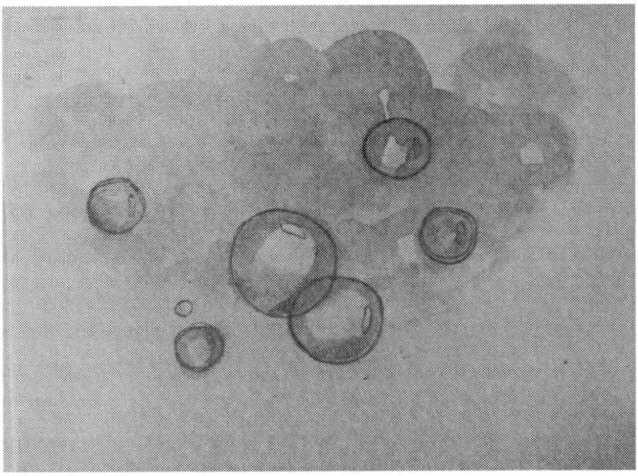

Why washings were; sometimes through hollow hole
Of pipe amused we blew, and sent aloft
The floating bubbles; little dreaming then
To see, Montgolfier[113], thy silken ball
Ride buoyant through the clouds, so near approach
The sports of children and the toils of men.
Earth, air, and sky, and ocean hath its bubbles,
And verse is one of them — this most of all.

113 Montgolfier: (n) the first hot air balloon to achieve free flight in France (1783)

"Washing Day" is a great example of poetry of sensibility, an expression of spontaneous feelings of the heart. In the last part of the 18th century, it poured from women's emotional experiences, from women who stood in the margins of culture. The aim of poetry of sensibility is to affect through sympathy and not by imitation. Women poets are sympathetic to distress and victimization with a profound emotion of being themselves dispossessed. In her poem, Anna Barbauld challenges male-dominated values by portraying an alienated sensibility through the description of daily chores.

The narrator gives us two separate viewpoints occurring during a day of washing. One view shows us the typical feelings women have doing the mundane chores of their day. The other is how the narrator views the chores through the eyes of a child, highlighting the joy and innocence of childhood juxtaposed against the harsh washing day of housewives.

The poem starts with an invocation of the muses, as epic poetry of old once did. Only this time, instead of giving inspiration, the Muses are gossiping since it is "dreaded Washing-Day." No one feels the toils of women can draw much inspiration like those of men. Women are prone to only gossip after all. The sarcasm is evident here. To highlight this, the first two-thirds of the poem reads like an epic, exaggerating the toils of a woman's day into nearly impossible tasks. Unlike the heroes of old, the women appear enslaved to their husbands, "the yoke of wedlock." Women feel like they have no choice in what their occupation will be, unlike men. They can only be housewives.

After breakfast, the narrator despairs over the cloudy sky promising rain. Rain will only soak the drying clothes further until they are heavy enough to snap the line, staining them again. She sarcastically references the ruined

morning as the "petty miseries of life." They may seem petty to the reader, but to the narrator and other women it is wearisome, difficult, and thankless work. Thankless because in later lines she thinks of the husband returning and adding more work, such as feeding him his meal or mending a sock. Still not understanding how much work there is to be done, the husband has the audacity to ask her to go for a walk! Her response is a blank look and the threat of him eating dinner alone. The housewife's is not a life to envy.

The narrator then shifts to a memory of washing day during her childhood, and the mood changes from annoyance to awe. As a child, she could not understand why the older women were irritated with her presence and drove her off. She remembers that the women would offer her sweets and fanciful stories on other days. Why not on this washing day? The child takes comfort with her grandmother and tries to understand why washing day is so stressful for everyone. She still cannot understand, even when she hears her mother's voice urging the women to work harder. There is much stress and tiredness in her voice. To the child, the bubbles from the wash basin are a wonder to behold.

The last few lines of the poem highlight the deeper themes of this poem. To the child, bubbles are fanciful, free from the labor that produced them. This is contrasted against the wonder of the Barbauld's generation, the hot air balloon created by Montgolfier and named after him. "The floating bubbles; little dreaming then / To see, Montgolfier, thy silken ball / Ride buoyant through the clouds / All the labors of men seem to be worth the effort put into them." The works of men are celebrated and displayed like the hot air balloon was. Thus, they make working over them important, make men important. Even the poetry men create seems to be worth the effort. But what about the toil of women? The laborious efforts of washing day? Who sings of this, or even makes poetry of it? No one, until now. The child is right in questioning why the wash is being done. "Then would I sit me down and ponder much / Why washings were." Why bother indeed. Yet, we all know the answer to the question. What would happen if our clothes were not cleaned?

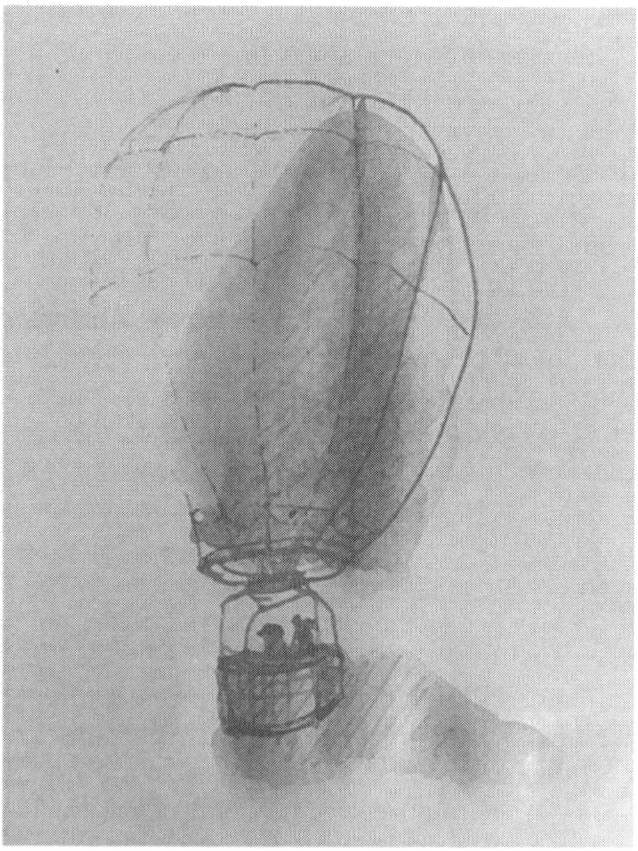

EIGHTEEN HUNDRED AND ELEVEN

Anna Laetitia Barbauld

Still the loud death drum, thundering from afar,
O'er the vext[114] nations pours the storm of war:
To the stern call still Britain bends her ear,
Feeds the fierce strife, the' alternate
hope and fear;
Bravely, though vainly, dares to strive with Fate,
And seeks by turns to prop each sinking state.
Colossal power with overwhelming force
Bears down each fort of Freedom in its course;
Prostrate she lies beneath the Despot's sway,
While the hushed nations curse him—and obey[115]

114 Vext: (v) archaic; past tense for vex, meaning to harass

115 Despot's sway...obey: a reference to Napoleon's policy to cut Great Britain off from continental Europe despite Britain's economic power at the time.

Bounteous in vain, with frantic man at strife,
Glad Nature pours the means—the joys of life;
In vain with orange-blossoms scents the gale,
The hills with olives clothes, with corn the vale;
Man calls to Famine, nor invokes in vain,
Disease and Rapine follow in her train;
The tramp of
marching hosts disturbs the plough,
The sword, not sickle, reaps the harvest now,
And where the soldier gleans the scant supply,
The helpless peasant but retires to die;
No laws his hut from licensed outrage shield,
And war's least horror is the' ensanguined field.
Fruitful in vain, the matron counts with pride
The blooming youths that grace her honoured side;
No son returns to press her widowed hand,
Her fallen blossoms strew a foreign strand.
—Fruitful in vain, she boasts her virgin race,

Whom cultured arts adorn and gentlest grace;
Defrauded of its homage, Beauty mourns,
And the rose withers on its virgin thorns.
Frequent, some stream obscure, some uncouth name,
By deeds of blood is lifted into fame;
Oft o'er the daily page some soft one bends
To learn the fate of husband, brothers, friends,
Or the spread map with anxious eye explores,
Its dotted boundaries and penciled shores,
Asks wherethe spot that wrecked her bliss is found,
And learns its name but to detest the sound.

And think'st thou, Britain, still to sit at ease,
An island queen amidst thy subject seas,
While the vext billows, in their distant roar,
But soothe thy slumbers, and but kiss thy shore?
To sport in wars, while danger keeps aloof,
Thy grassy turf unbruised by hostile hoof?
So sing thy flatterers;—but, Britain, know,
Thou who hast shared the guilt must share the woe.
Nor distant is the hour; low murmurs spread,
And whispered fears, creating what they dread;
Ruin, as with an earthquake shock, is here,
There, the heart-witherings of unuttered fear,
And that sad death, whence most affection bleeds,
Which sickness, only of the soul, precedes.
Thy baseless wealth dissolves in air away,
Like mists that melt before the morning ray:
No more on crowded mart or busy street
Friends, meeting friends, with cheerful hurry greet;
Sad, on the ground thy princely merchants bend
Their altered looks, and evil days portend,
And fold their arms, and watch with anxious breast
The tempest blackening in the distant West.

Yet, O my Country, name beloved, revered,
By every tie that binds the soul endeared,
Whose image to my infant senses came
Mixt with Religion's light and Freedom's holy flame!
If prayers may not avert, if 'tis thy fat
To rank amongst the names that once were great,
Not like the dim, cold
Crescent shalt thou fade,
Thy debt to Science and the
Muse unpaid;
Thine are the laws
surrounding states revere,
Thine the full harvest of the
mental year,
Thine the bright stars in
Glory's sky that shine,
And arts that make it life to live are thine.
If westward streams the light that leaves thy shores,
Still from thy lamp the streaming radiance pours.

....

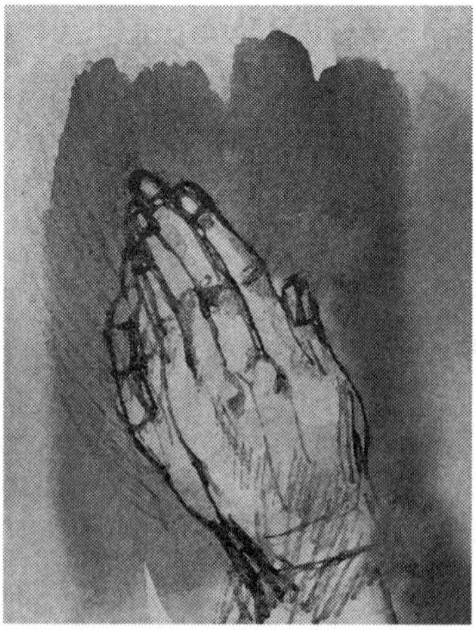

England, the seat of arts, be only known
By the grey ruin and the mouldering stone;
That Time may tear the garland from her brow,
And Europe sit in dust, as Asia now.

Yet then the' ingenuous youth whom Fancy fires
With pictured glories of illustrious sires,
With duteous zeal their pilgrimage shall take
From the Blue Mountains, or Ontario's lake,

....

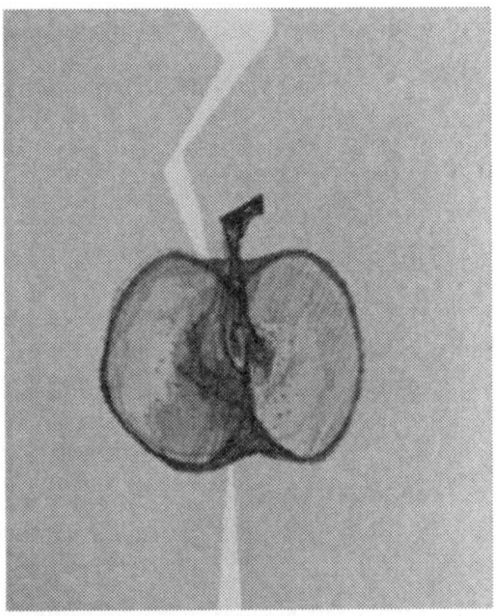

But fairest flowers expand but to decay;
The worm is in thy core, thy glories pass away;
Arts, arms and wealth destroy the fruits they bring;
Commerce, like beauty, knows no second spring.
Crime walks thy streets, Fraud earns her unblest bread,
O'er want and woe thy gorgeous robe is spread,
And angel charities in vain oppose:
With grandeur's growth the mass of misery grows.
For see,—to other climes the

Genius soars,
He turns from Europe's desolated shores;
And lo, even now, midst mountains wrapt in storm,
On Andes' heights he shrouds his awful form;
On Chimborazo's[116] summits treads sublime,
Measuring in lofty thought the march of Time;
Sudden he calls:—"'Tis now the hour!" he cries,
Spreads his broad hand, and bids the nations rise.
La Plata[117] hears amidst her torrents' roar;
Potosi[118] hears it, as she digs the ore:
Ardent, the Genius[119] fans the noble strife,
And pours through feeble souls a higher life,
Shouts to the mingled tribes from sea to sea,
And swears—Thy world, Columbus, shall be free.

116 Chimborazo: the highest mountain in Equador

117 La Plata: a river in Uruguay, South America, that flows into the Atlantic Ocean

118 Potosi: a city in Bolivia, South America, famous for its silver mines

119 Genius: an entity that determines fate, makes history move, and causes empires to rise and fall

Since "Eighteen Hundred and Eleven, a Poem" was written during the Napoleonic Wars, it begins in the midst of a battle. Britain had been at war with Napoleon's France for ten years and was on the brink of losing. Napoleon had instituted a policy of isolationism where Europe was to cut all trade with Britain. Plus, Britain's 220,000-man army was no match for France's million-man army. The only advantage Britain had to sustain itself against such odds was its navy's superiority. The overall mood of the poem is dark and creates a feeling of defeat, with phrases like "death drum" and "storm of war". Unlike other war poetry of the time that celebrated bravery and victory, Barbauld's poem suggests that there are no victors in war since so many people suffer and die because of it. "Bounteous in vain, with frantic man at strife." In fact, in the section presented here, Barbauld uses "vain" seven times, repeating the idea that such armed strife against France was pointless when compared to the loss of life. By 1811, Barbauld had had enough of empire and war.

The second and third stanza laments the death and destruction of both humanity and nature which were "bounteous in vain." She fills her poem with images of flowers to signify the fall of the British empire and the rise of a nation of individuals in its place. She does this in a rather clever way. Though she writes, "orange-blossoms scent the gale," she juxtaposes this natural beauty with "Famine…Disease and Rapine." Thus, by the time we get to the third stanza, Britain's orange blossoms, or "blooming youths", become instead "her fallen blossoms." War and empire cannot justify the loss of life in Barbauld's opinion.

Britain was the largest industrial nation in the world and a world-wide empire at the time Barbauld wrote this poem. She recognizes this with some rather brief images, but such glory will not last. She states, "That Time may tear the garland from her brow, / And Europe sit in dust, as Asia now." Thus, the tearing of the garland (a reference to a crown) from England's brow becomes the fall of the British Empire. All that England once controlled will be reduced to a "dim, cold crescent."

When one empire falls another must arise, and Barbauld foresaw the rise of a young country far in the Americas. The bands of flowers are to be passed to "the ingenuous youth whom Fancy fires / With pictured glories of illustrious sires, / With duteous zeal their pilgrimage shall take / From the Blue Mountains or Ontario's lake." Though the symbolism is a bit vague, if you know where the Blue Mountains (in Oregon in the west) and Ontario's lake (New York in the east) is, then it's clear she is referencing the United States. She also calls the American's pilgrims, those who fled England in the 17th century because of religious persecution and founded the American colonies.

It will not be the master of nations (England) who will rule the world, but the master of nature. To Barbauld, industrialization had corrupted England. "The worm is in thy core, thy glories pass away." Thus, the Genius through the final lines of the poem paint a picture of the pristine Americas (both North and South) untouched by the ruination of continental war and industrialization.

A Brief Introduction to Amelia Opie

(1769-1853)

Known mostly for her novels, Amelia (Alderson) Opie was a poet at heart. As a teenager, she had written mostly poetry and was published in several journals, most notably in the *Monthly Magazine*. Born in Norwich to parents of staunch Unitarian faith, Amelia received only a minimal education. Her father, a reputable physician, was well known for his radical ideas in politics as well as charity toward poorer patients. The death of Amelia's mother in 1784 forced Amelia to take charge of the household at the age of 15. Many of her poems refer to her mother, albeit in an unflattering manner, concentrating mostly on her ways of reproving and disciplining Amelia.

Her mother's death forced Amelia to bloom into a socialite to host parties for her well-to-do father. She furthered her popularity by composing and singing ballads for her guests. By 1794, she began making annual trips to London, included herself into many literary circles, and associated with the likes of Mary Wollstonecraft. In 1797, amidst many suitors, Amelia met John Opie, a painter, and married him in 1798. He is known to have encouraged her to write but more so out of his disdain for society life. In 1801, she became a professional writer with the publication of *Father and Daughter: A Tale*, although she did publish earlier under an anonymous name. Within this successful novel, she wrote a gem of a poem "The Maid of Corinth."

She followed her sophomore novel by publishing two volumes of poetry. In 1802, she published *An Elegy to the Memory of the Duke of Bedford and Poems*, which contained two of her most popular poems, "The Orphan Boy" and "The Felon's Address to his Child". The sudden success of the latter volume lasted for nine years where it was reprinted into its sixth edition. She followed these volumes with *The Warriors Return, and Other Poems* in 1808.

Suffering from depression, Amelia's husband returned to Norwich and died from swelling of the brain in 1807. To alleviate her own depression, Amelia converted to Quakerism in 1814, which ended her novel writing, but increased her charity. In support of anti-slavery, she wrote "The Black Man's Lament" in 1826. Her last book of poetry, *Lays for the Dead*, was published in 1834. Considered to be perhaps her best volume of poetry, she lamented the death of loved ones in simplistic verse.

BLACK MAN'S LAMENT

Amelia Opie

Come, listen to my plaintive ditty[120],
Ye tender hearts, and children dear!
And, should it move souls to pity,
Oh! try to *end* the griefs you hear.

There is a beauteous plant, that grows
In western India's sultry clime,
Which makes, alas! the Black man's woes,
And also makes the White man's crime.

For know, its tall gold stems contain
A sweet rich juice, which White men prize;
And that they may this *sugar* gain,
The Negro toils, and bleeds, and dies.

120 ditty: (n) a poem meant to be sung

But, Negro slave! *thyself* shall tell,
Of past and present wrongs the story;
And would all British hearts could feel,
To end those wrongs were Britain's glory.
Negro speaks

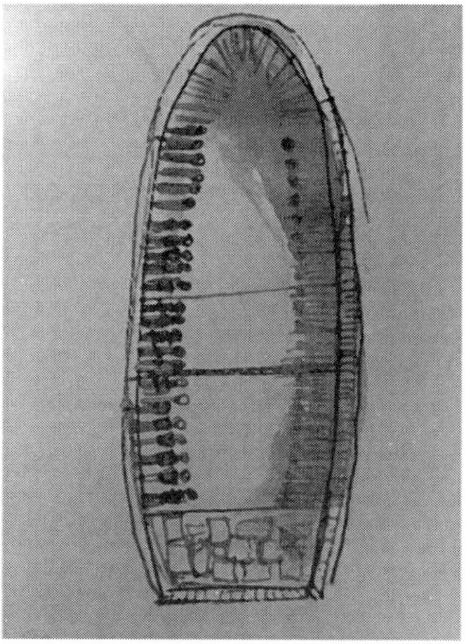

First to our own dear Negro land,
His ships the cruel White man sends;
And there contrives, by armed band,
To tear us from our homes and friends;

From parents, brethren's fond embrace;
From tender wife, and child to tear;
Then in a darksome ship to place,
Pack'd close, like bales of cotton there.

Oh! happy those, who, in that hour,
Die from their prison's putrid breath!
Since they escape from White man's pow'r,
From toils and stripes, and lingering death!
For what awaited us on shore,
Soon as the ship had reach'd the strand,
Unloading its degraded store
Of freemen, forc'd from Negro land?

See! eager White men come around,
To choose and claim us for their slaves;
And make us envy those who found
In the dark ship their early graves.

They bid black men and women stand
In lines, the drivers in the rear:
Poor Negroes hold a hoe in hand,
But they the wicked cart-whip bear.

Then we, in gangs, like beasts in droves,
Swift to the cane-fields driven are;
There first our toil the weeds removes,
And next we holes for plants prepare.
But woe to all, both old and young,
Women and men, or strong or weak,
Worn out or fresh, those gangs among,
That dare the toilsome line to break!

………………

He ceas'd; for here his tears would flow,
And ne'er resum'd his tale of ruth.
Alas! it rends my heart to know
He only told a tale of truth.

Amelia Opie was aware of the plight of African slaves in the British colonies at the beginning of the 19th century. Opie, a **Quaker**, opposed the slave trade by campaigning actively for its end. “Black Man’s Lament” (1802) is one of several influential abolitionist poems.

In this poem, Opie skillfully positions us to witness the tragedy of becoming a slave through the juxtaposition of the two speakers. The first is an educated colonial poet while the second is a slave from the West Indies, aptly forcing us to enter the slavery debate as an active participant. We see firsthand the horrors of the slave trade. The poem was originally illustrated to better assist educating children while reading the poem. The philosophical implications were for the benefit of the adult readers who needed to understand the plight of the slave.

The 172-verse poem is divided into two parts. The first sixteen verses are spoken through an educated English poet, who introduces the plight of the black slaves. It is a clever device to allow the predominantly white readers of the time to trust what the poet was saying before switching points of view. The remainder of the poem is an account of a black slave’ s experience harvesting sugar cane in the West Indies (the Caribbean islands).

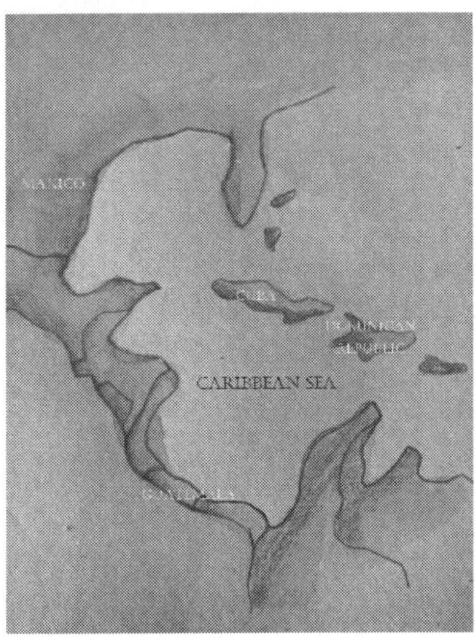

The educated poet starts off juxtaposing the beauty of the sugar cane plants with the pity of the black slaves. The weather of the islands is excellent for growing such a wonderous plant, but it causes the natives' suffering through the white man's exploitation. The mistreatment of the black natives to obtain the precious sugar only leads to death and suffering. However, the British readers could not possibly be moved by a white man's account of such oppression since it is too impersonal; therefore, a black slave will give his tale and especially try to nudge the British people to bring an end to slavery.

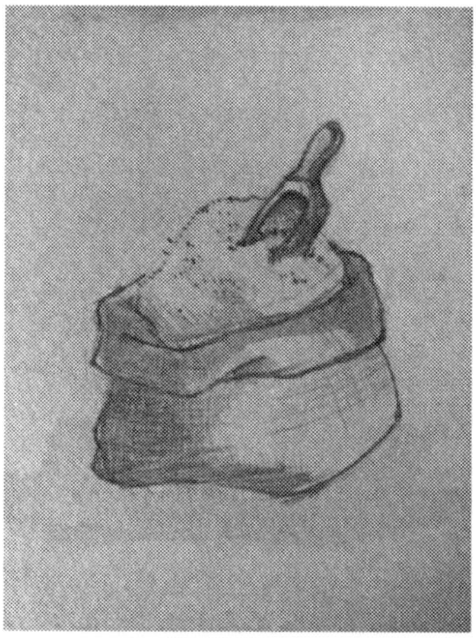

The slave starts his lament with a heart wrenching description of how he was torn from his family by white slavers and stuffed onto a ship like bales of cotton. The stench and horrid conditions of the journey were so bad that those who died before entering the ship were better off, since death was the only way to escape the white slavers' cruelty. Once unloaded in a new land, the degradation only got worse.

The **metaphor** changes from the slaves being a plant-like product to a more beast-like workforce. The slave suffers being sold like cattle to more cruel slavers. He is made to dig holes to plant the sugar cane plant, but the only motivation to work is being whipped as a horse is whipped pulling a cart. This line gives a sharp reality to the slave's condition. There is no reward for doing the white man's work, only suffering. Not only he, but young and old, male and female, all must suffer the cruelest treatment. The slave eventually breaks down in tears, failing to finish his tale. So horrible is his suffering that it leaves the otherwise loquacious poet speechless, and the poem ends with the same effect on the reader.

PART II

ELEMENTS OF POETRY

From the beginning of civilization, people have tried to give expression to the world they experience. This is often done with some type of rhythm called poetry. It is the most significant expression of thoughts brought forth into the spoken word. What makes poetry great is that it expresses ideas and feelings in ways that others can relate to. It gives thoughts a type of form. The poet must choose the right words to make these images concrete. Milton found poetry to be "simple, sensuous, and impassioned."

The first function of poetry is to please the senses. Poets explain sights, sound, and colors in ways that produce these images in the reader's minds. This is often accomplished in a musical form. Poetry is found in every aspect of creative expression: in songs, dramas, stories, myths, even in modern popular music. No one can resist its attraction. A life without poetry of any kind is life without enjoyment.

Thus, poetry is an art form that increases in pleasure the more you study the form. Words on a blank page are like colored paint on a canvas—anyone can do it—but only the true artist can do it well. When you walk into a museum to view a Jackson Pollock painting, you may wonder what makes it art, and you may wonder correctly. You may open this book and read William Carlos Williams's "Red Wheelbarrow", then wonder why it is poetry. You may also think that anyone can write a poem like that. The answer to that response is that anyone *can* write poetry if that person truly understands the elements of poetry.

Reading this text will help you explore five different elements of poetry that are used by the poet to make verse richer and more fulfilling. When you finish this section, hopefully you will never look at a published poem and ask, "Why is this a poem?" You will better appreciate the art form that is poetry, and every reading will enrich your life. Perhaps you will even start to write poetry yourself.

ELEMENT ONE: DICTION

Poetry is like a feast of words. If we are to attend a banquet, how boring it would be to feast upon the same old dish and flavor time and again. A feast means that we satisfy ourselves on a variety of flavors and textures. Poets are the same as chefs at a banquet, struggling over the perfect dish. Poets test, combine, and stress over each word written on the page. Nothing gets past their scrutiny. To enjoy and experience the craft of the poet, we must slow down and savor the language the poet has so tirelessly written for our pleasure. Would we sit down at a banquet and quickly eat the food? Or would we simply sit and enjoy the menagerie of flavors the chefs had cooked for us? Poetry is the same. Give it patience and you will be rewarded with some of the best-crafted language in history.

Diction has traditionally been recognized as language with a natural poetic excellence that stands out from the common usage. Some common words deemed poetical are "betwixt" meaning "between" and "art" meaning "are," and are only found in poems. Though this was the case before the 19th century, the romantic poets with Wordsworth at the head wanted to bridge the gap "betwixt" this so-called poetic style of speech and everyday spoken language, which led to poetic diction becoming more "down to earth" or regular in execution. In contemporary poetry, such archaic style of diction is used for an ironic effect, affording the poet a wider template of language.

In reading poetry, we not only need to know the meaning of the words but also what they imply. Words contain both denotations and connotations. The **denotation** is the meaning found in the dictionary. It is rather dull on its own, like all the separate ingredients in the kitchen, not very appetizing. If I say the word "wine," the denotation is "fermented juice of grapes." That is a dull way of looking at the word. However, the **connotation**, or the emotional idea or attitude of the word, is more romantic since wine is used during candlelit dinners. It also conjures up religious images of the blood of Christ as hinted at during the Last Supper and used in Catholic mass. Thus, the connotation carries the most significance in the reading of words. When all the ingredients or words are combined, then the mundane denotations give way to a feast of connotations, which are what you need to focus on more in reading poetry.

Since poets do not write anything except those words that work best for the poem, we must understand how these words add to feelings, and what is implied in the words instead of what is meant. Thus, we must get into the habit of reading for both the denotation and connotation of the words. Let's examine Alfred, Lord Tennyson's "The Eagle":

THE EAGLE

Alfred, Lord Tennyson

He clasps the crag with crooked hands;
Close to the sun in lonely lands,
Ringed with the azure world, he stands.
The wrinkled sea beneath him crawls;
He watches from his mountain walls,
And like a thunderbolt he falls.

First, as an astute reader, we need to look at the word "hands." Why does the speaker use a human word for a bird? Why not use "talons"? If we read only the denotation, then the meaning can be confusing. However, what the connotation conjures in our minds is quite different. Lord Tennyson is **personifying** the regal creature and giving it a more human characteristic; thus, what happens to the eagle has direct consequences to humanity as well. This is further emphasized by starting the poem with the masculine/human form of "he".

The use of the nouns in the poem are rather simplistic: "hands", "lands", "world", "sea", and "walls." However, what creates **concrete imagery** are the adjectives next to these nouns. "Crooked" could easily be replaced by "bent" or "curved." However, the use of "crooked" suggests several acceptable denotations. According to the *Oxford English Dictionary*, "crooked" could mean "bent or twisted; a deformed person; dishonest or corrupt." With any of these definitions the meaning of the poem can change or transform. That is the denotation. What about the connotations?

"Crooked hands" suggest malformed hands or even hands of an elderly man, perhaps the hands of a once mighty king bent with age. Another word that stands out is "azure." The denotation is a bright blue color; "pertaining to a sea-god; cloudless; or serene." The connotation invokes a blue world of majesty that the eagle rules over with "mountain walls" being synonymous with castle walls. How would the connotation change if it was written as "blue world"? In fact, let's change the connotation of the whole poem without changing the denotation by using synonyms (of course rhyme and meter will be broken, but that will not concern us here):

It grabs the cliff with curved claws;
Close to the sun in lost areas,
Enclosed in the blue sky, it stands.
The undulating sea below moves;
It watches from its mountain face,
And like a rock it plummets.

The poem keeps the denotative meaning of the poem accurately; however, ignoring the rhyme and meter change, the connotation of the poet is not only completely transformed, it further becomes base and common.

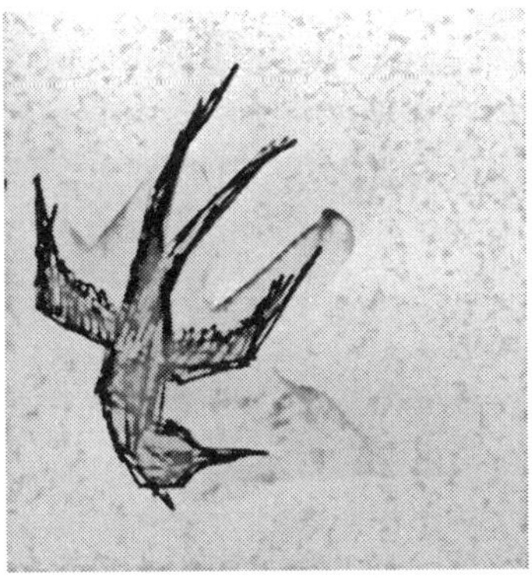

Finally, in the last stanza are the words "thunderbolt" and "falls." Both words are incongruent. A thunderbolt connotes a form of power, the influence of the gods, stately. However, "falls" connotes a form of inanimation. Not only does it conjure images of a rock falling, but also the Biblical Fall, as a person of high stature reduced to nothing. We could easily read it as an eagle launching from its perch on the mountain ledge and is dropping like a thunderbolt down to some unsuspecting prey below. However, if we choose to take all the connotations in the poem together

—the personification, the royalty of the bird's domain, the mountainous, fortress-like walls of its perch—then another connotation comes to light. We could easily read that someone has shot the poor bird and it suddenly plummets to its death, like a thunderbolt striking the earth, reminding the reader that not only the majesty of nature, but of all humanity, is frail and precariously so. Through understanding **diction**, the interpretation of this poem shows that nature can consume all things on a whim, but we, humans, can consume it quicker and more effortlessly.

Myth also inspires feelings of awe that often brings about certain understandings called **epiphany**, an enlightening revelation. For John Keats (1795-1821), who had already read Homer's *Iliad* and *Odyssey* translated into **free verse** form or dry heroic couplets, an epiphany struck when he encountered the Elizabethan playwright George Chapman' s translation of Homer's epics in lively verse. This was at a time when only the original language of such poetry was considered meaningful and translations were but boorish attempts at art. Impressed with classical themes and images, Keats sat down and penned his own response to Chapman's translations in his own heroic verse.

ON FIRST LOOKING INTO CHAPMAN'S HOMER

John Keats (1795-1821)

Much have I travelled in the realms of gold,
And many goodly states and kingdoms seen;
Round many western islands have I been
Which bards in fealty to Apollo[1] hold.
Oft of one wide expanse had I been told
That deep-browed Homer[2] ruled as his demesne;[3]
Yet did I never breathe its pure serene
Till I heard Chapman speak out loud and bold:
Then felt I like some watcher of the skies
When a new planet[4] swims into his ken;[5]
Or like stout Cortez[6] when with eagle eyes
He stared at the Pacific — and all his men
Looked at each other with a wild surmise —
Silent, upon a peak in Darien.[7]

1 Apollo: The Greek and Roman god of poetry

2 Homer: 9th century B.C. Greek poet of the *Iliad* and *Odyssey*

3 demesne: (n) a district or region

4 new planet: Neptune

5 ken: (n) knowledge

6 Cortez: Hernan Cortez (1485-1547), a Spanish explorer; however, was not the first to see the Pacific; credit is given to a less famous Spanish explorer Balboa

7 Darien: a mountain in eastern Panama, Central America

Again, how does do you shout out to the world such an epiphany as finding poetic creativity of classical ideas in the vulgar English language? You respond in kind. Keats explores his emotions outside the everyday usage and moves into the mythic to show the reader just what it is like to experience the divine in words. The first half of the poem is Keats's attempt to express his appreciation for all "the realms of gold" that he has read and that he has read a lot. Out of all that he has read, Homer is considered one of the finest storytellers, but not until Keats has experienced Chapman's translation, has he ever felt such elation. Keats recalls the discovery of Neptune, the "new planet," and how this changed the field of science at his time, and still his discovery of Chapman's Homer cannot even begin to compare with the elations of that. He talks of the emotions Spanish Cortez and how his men must have felt when they reached the Pacific Ocean—although Keats is mistaken for it was another explorer. Keats' historical mistake is forgiven in context of his mythmaking. He is like a man discovering God for the first time. Oh, the rapture!

In opposition to the epic mythical view of life as found in Keats's poetry is the quiet everyday usage of language that basically deals with the same themes. Keats uses grandiose themes and language to create **concrete images** of immaterial ideas. On the other hand, we can see that the simple language of life is just as effective as the mythic—it's just a little quieter but no less effective .

IT IS A BEAUTEOUS EVENING

William Wordsworth (1770-1850)

It is a beauteous evening, calm and free,
The holy time is quiet as a Nun
Breathless with adoration; the broad sun
Is sinking down in its tranquility;
The gentleness of heavens broods o'er the Sea:
Listen! the mighty Being[8] is awake,
And doth with his eternal motion make
A sound like thunder — everlastingly.
Dear Child! dear Girl! that walkest with me here,
If thou appear untouched by solemn thought,
Thy nature is not therefore less divine:
Thou liest in Abraham's bosom[9] all the year,
And worship'st at the Temple's inner shrine,
God being with thee when we know it not.

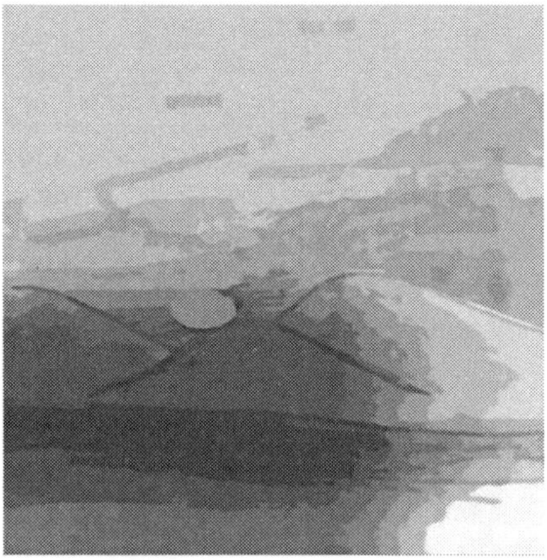

8 mighty Being: God

9 Abraham's bosom: Heaven

Wordsworth's "It Is a Beauteous Evening" gives us a glimpse into the everyday. Here the narrator is walking on a beach with his daughter, enjoying the quiet sunset. "The holy time is quiet as a Nun / Breathless with adoration." In his description of the sunset, Wordsworth invokes Catholic images that make it seem they are walking in a cathedral, except this one is not manmade but devised by God. In fact, God is there in the natural altar that is the sea, living and exerting his influence upon the land. "Listen! The Mighty Being is awake, / And doth with his eternal motion make / A sound like thunder—everlastingly." It is here that the narrator and daughter enjoy a stroll. While the narrator takes in the significance of man and nature, his daughter probably does not. That does not matter, however, for she, like all children, rest in "Abraham's bosom" (a very Christian **metaphor** for heaven) all year long. Adults must go out of their way to experience God in nature; for children, God is with them always and need not to contemplate the wonders of their surroundings.

THE SECOND COMING

W.B. Yeats

Turning and turning in the widening gyre
The falcon cannot hear the falconer;
Things fall apart; the center cannot hold;
Mere anarchy is loosed upon the world,
The blood-dimmed tide is loosed, and everywhere
The ceremony of innocence is drowned;
The best lack all conviction, while the worst
Are full of passionate intensity.

Surely some revelation is at hand;
Surely the Second Coming is at hand.
The Second Coming! Hardly are those words out
When a vast image out of *Spritus Mundi*
Troubles my sight: somewhere in sands of the desert
A shape with lion body and the head of a man[10],
A gaze blank and pitiless as the sun,
Is moving its slow thighs, while all about it
Reel shadows of the indignant desert birds.
The darkness drops again; but now I know
That twenty centuries of stony sleep
were vexed to nightmare by a rocking cradle,
And what rough beast, its hour come round at last,
Slouches towards Bethlehem to be born?

---

10 A sphinx

W.B. Yeats had a somewhat darker approach to religion than Wordsworth. With Wordsworth there was hope. Even though Wordsworth had lost faith in the future of humanity after the French Revolution turned from individualism back to an empire, he knew there was a purpose to everything that all of humanity needed to gain experience. For Yeats, he had lost all hope for his Age. Being Irish, he was disenchanted by British colonial rule and witnessed the blatant destruction and horror of World War I. In "The Second Coming," Yeats sees the ideals of Christianity being well on their way out of practice as a falcon continues to circle wider and wider, having lost sight of its master until entirely lost.

The first stanza speaks of the way the narrator views the world, a world of anarchy and loss of innocence. The second stanza intones the need for revelation, the much anticipated Second Coming of Christ, perhaps. However, as all things in the past, the old must give way to the new. The *Spiritus Mundi* that he sees as the soul of the world has taken on the shape of a horrible sphinx, "A shape with lion body and the head of a man," and instead of the promised light of the world coming, darkness and shadows follow. Just as the dove announced the birth of a Christian age, desert birds, buzzards most likely for they feed on death, announce the opening of this new age that, for Yeats, ended after World War I.

Instead of the Christ child born in the manger "twenty centuries" ago, a new "Messiah" now "Slouches towards Bethlehem to be born." What this beast was to be, we may never know. Thank goodness Yeats wasn't speaking prophetically but allegorically. We get a sense of nihilism that was common during this age of depression and war, where many had lost hope in religion to bring them out of the darkness and turned, instead, to despair.

ELEMENT TWO: SYNTAX

If **diction** is vocabulary, one word at a time, then **syntax** is best explained as how the words are arranged in any given sentence. Poetry is well suited for the rearrangement of syntax. While the vocabulary can be common and easy to understand, the syntax found in poetry can lead to misunderstanding and confusion, especially for students learning English as another language. A good example for analysis is W.B. Yeats's poem "The Lake Isle of Innisfree".

THE LAKE ISLE OF INNISFREE

William Butler Yeats (1865-1939)

I will arise and go now, and go to Innisfree,[11]
And a small cabin build there, of clay and wattles[12] made:
Nine bean-rows will I have there, a hive for the honey-bee,
And live alone in the bee-loud glade.

And I shall have some peace there, for peace comes dropping slow,
Dropping from the veils of the morning to where the cricket sings;
There midnight's all a glimmer, and noon a purple glow,
And evening full of the linnet's[13] wings.

I will arise and go now, for always night and day
I hear lake water lapping[14] with low sounds by the shore;
While I stand on the roadway, or on the pavements grey,
I hear it in the deep heart's core.

---

11 Innisfree: located in Ireland

12 wattle: (n) sticks interwoven together to make a wall

13 linnet: (n) a small bird

14 lap: (v) water washing up against something

The poem starts with uncommon syntax. "I will arise and go now, and go to Innisfree, / And a small cabin build there, of clay and wattles made." We would not encounter such a structure in prose unless the writer was also trying to be poetic. A more common way to write the sentence is "I will arise and go now to Innisfree and build a small clay and wattles cabin." Obviously, the latter sentence is not as creative as Yeats's.

The reason why Yeats changes the syntax to an unorthodox structure is to manipulate the tone and give us a glimpse into the speaker's state of mind. The repetition of "go" reveals how the speaker is feeling; there is a sense of urgency for leaving, dissatisfaction over the current status quo. This is similar to how we may speak to a friend on the phone. The conversation is going on too long, and we feel urgency in stopping the call and moving on. We may speak as thus: "I've gotta go now, gotta go to the store before it closes." The repetition not only reveals our state of urgency, but also our need to excuse ourselves from the present predicament.

In the second line, Yeats changes the syntax completely to describe the cabin. One of the obvious reasons is to shift focus onto the cabin, which is the heart of the stanza. It is interesting to note that the object of the sentence comes before the verbs. Poets use this form of passive voice to downplay who is responsible for something. Here the speaker wishes to emphasize the cabin and what it is built of, not who built it. He also rearranges the syntax to meet the meter of thirteen syllables per line that he has established for the first three lines of each stanza.

Another common type of poetic syntax is the **ellipsis**, or leaving words out of sentences where the reader usually expects to read them. For example, in "Preludes"

by T.S. Eliot, the poet utilizes ellipsis to keep meter in his poem: “You curled the papers from **your** hair, / Or clasped the yellow soles of feet / In the palms of both soiled hands.” I emphasized “your” in the first line. Can you see where ellipsis is used in the following lines? “Your” is omitted in the following two lines. Correct grammar would be written as “*your* feet” and “*your* soiled hands.”

Thomas Hardy’s “The Darkling Thrush” is another good example of utilizing ellipsis.

THE DARKLING THRUSH

Thomas Hardy

I leant upon a coppice gate
When Frost was specter-gray,
And Winter's dregs made desolate
The weakening eye of day.

The tangled bine-stems scored the sky
Like strings of broken lyres,
And all mankind that haunted nigh
Had sought their household fires.

The land's sharp features seemed to be
The Century's corpse outleant,
His crypt the cloudy canopy,
The wind his death-lament.
The ancient pulse of germ and birth
Was shrunken hard and dry,
And every spirit upon earth
Seemed fervorless as I.

At once a voice arose among
The bleak twigs overhead
In a full-hearted evensong
Of joy illimited;
An aged thrush, frail, gaunt, and small,
In blast-beruffled plume,
Had chosen thus to fling his soul
Upon the growing gloom.

So little cause for carolings

Of such ecstatic sound
Was written on terrestrial things
Afar or nigh around,
That I could think there trembled through
His happy good-night air
Some blessèd Hope, whereof he knew
And I was unaware.

Let's take a closer look at the third stanza. There are features in the first line that can be repeated in the last two lines. The form "seemed to be" is used to link the first line to the second. Ellipsis is used to omit the grammatical feature to create conciseness without losing meaning. The third and fourth line should read, "His crypt *seemed to be* the cloudy canopy, / The wind *seemed to be* his death-lament."

Let's look at Robert Frost's poem "The Silken Tent" for another example of syntax used for poetic means.

THE SILKEN TENT

Robert Frost

She is as in a field a silken tent
At midday when the sunny summer breeze
Has dried the dew and all its ropes relent,[15]
So that in guys[16] it gently sways at ease,
And its supporting central cedar pole,
That is its pinnacle to heavenward
And signifies the sureness of the soul,
Seems to owe naught[17] to any single cord,
But strictly held by none, is loosely bound
By countless silken ties of love and thought
To everything on earth the compass round,[18]
And only by one's going slightly taut
In the capriciousness[19] of summer air
Is of the slightest bondage made aware.

15 relent: (v) slacken

16 guy: (n) a rope used to secure a tent

17 naught: (n) nothing

18 the compass round: in every direction on the compass; north, east, south, and west

19 capriciousness: (n) erratic; directionless

An obvious form of syntax for this poem is that it is one **compound-complex sentence**. Look at the poem again and notice there are only commas at the end the lines and the period is not used until the last line. How does Frost make the poem comprehensible as one sentence? He uses the conjunctions *so* (line 4), *and* (line 5), *And* (line 7), *But* (line 9), as well as *And* (line 12). Using these conjunctions allows the reader to move from one clause to the next without losing context or understanding. The first three lines make a complex sentence connected by the subordinator *when* and is straightforward to understand. The complexity comes in lines 4-14. Line 4 continues the previous complex sentence with the subordinator *So that* with "it gently sways at ease" as the clause to follow. Line 5 uses *And* to create another independent clause with "its supporting central cedar pole" being the subject of the clause with the main verb "seems" not appearing until line 8, while line 6 and 7 serve only as an adjective clause. Frost reverses the syntax of line 13 and 14 to maintain the final rhyming couplet. It should correctly read, "In the capriciousness of summer air is made aware of the slightest bondage."

Finally, syntax in poetry is the poet's ability to break the sentences into discrete parts. Traditional poetry was more conventional, but the way poets punctuate and break the lines of their poems is not really understood. How a poet writes a poem is just as important as the meaning. Let's look at Lord Tennyson's "The Eagle" again to see the various ways it can be written. The first two lines are straight-forward.

He clasps the crag with crooked hands;
Close to the sun in lonely lands,

These lines paint a very clear picture of an eagle

standing on a cliff, high in the sky. Notice the ellipsis in the second line. It should read, "He stands close to the sun in lonely lands." The poet could change the punctuation to affect the overall meaning of the poem:

he clasps the crag... with crooked hands?
Close to the sun in lonely lands.

Though the words in the poem haven't changed, the meaning has by adding a bit of humor and maybe even **irony** through use of **ellipsis**, and the inclusion of a question mark at the end of the first line to replace the semicolon. With the capitals removed, the style of the poem is also altered into a more non-traditional form as is common with William Carlos Williams. The question mark also actively involves the reader to interpret the eagle's actions by agreeing or disagreeing with the speaker's suggestion that the eagle may or may not have crooked hands. It draws attention to the personification of the bird and questions the speaker' s overall usage of such a **metaphor** in a light or humorous way. The poem's syntax can be altered in a different way as well.

He clasps the crags
With "crooked hands;"
Close to the sun
In lonely lands!

The two lines have now been turned into four. The placing of quotations around "crooked hands" adds a moniker to the eagle as if this is unique to only this bird. The insertion of the exclamation mark at the end of the poem adds a surprise that both the speaker and reader share, the fact that there is nothing in the air or land for the regal bird to hunt.

As you can see, the syntactic style of a poem can change the overall meaning as well. We, as conscientious readers, need to pay closer attention to the syntax structures on the page to help our overall interpretation of the poem. This is what makes poetry much more fluid and exciting than prose.

A Brief Introduction to William Carlos Williams

(1883-1963)

Williams was a pediatrician who happened to like to write poetry on his prescription pads during his spare time. He was inspired by Ezra Pound, whom he went to school with, and his early poetry is highly influenced by the Imagism movement. With Pound's encouragement, Williams started publishing his poetry even while he still practiced medicine. Williams's poetry masters colloquial speech while creating the natural rhythm of American speech. This is in direct opposition to the iambic pentameter verse that most English poetry had used from the Renaissance up through the Victorian era. Being a family doctor helped him see and express the world through the eyes of everyday people, especially the modern city and town life.

Williams loved to create verse about objects and not about ideas. While Ezra Pound and T.S. Eliot focused on the harsh reality of modern life, Williams decided to focus on the everyday objects that occupy people's lives. He published his greatest collection of poems in *Spring and All* in 1922, but Eliot's publication of *The Wasteland* around the same time took all the focus away from what Wil-

liams had produced. His was a lighter dose of modernism. Like Pound, though, Williams was able to put into words a simple snapshot of the everyday and make it a work of art.

Williams even wrote **epic** poetry as Pound and Eliot did. However, the reader of Eliot and Pound must have a classical knowledge of literature or be lost in all the metaphors. Williams, on the other hand, wrote his epic poetry for the general reader. *Paterson* (1946-1958) is an epic poem in five volumes. It is a celebration of his hometown of Paterson, New Jersey, mixing different media of literature: poetic lyrics, prose, letters, autobiography, newspapers, and history. Because he kept his lines short, the pages of his epic volumes are full of white spaces. This recalls the themes of open road and isolation in American literature. The journey through America is open to all citizens, rich or poor, and the scenery offered to them is a mystery to be opened with each turn of the road, as what he reveals with each turn of the page. William Carlos Williams may have had a day job as a physician, but he was clearly no amateur in poetry.

When he was 65, he suffered from a heart attack. This greatly affected his health and he continued to have strokes the following year. After his death at the age of 79, he was awarded posthumously the Pulitzer Prize for his final book of poetry, *Pictures from Brueghel and Other Poems* (1962).

RED WHEEL BARROW

William Carlos Williams

so much depends
upon

a red wheel
barrow

glazed with rain
water

beside the white
chickens.

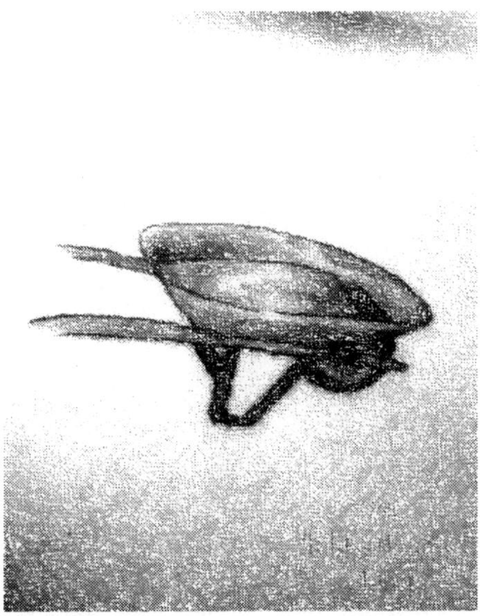

This poem looks quite different; it does not use capital letters at the beginning of the lines, nor does it follow any set rhythm or meter. Any careful reader, however, may start to notice that this poem does have structure. Williams himself said: "No verse can be free; it must be governed by some measure, but not by the old measure. We have to return to a measure consonant with our time [...] a purely intuitive one which we feel but do not name." The obvious structure is one sentence broken into four equal stanzas. Each stanza has only two lines with exactly three words on the first and only one word on the second. The structure of the poem is also connected to the theme, which is mentioned in each stanza. Farming is dependent upon farming implements like the red wheel barrow, rain, and the animals on the farm such as chickens. Far from being a nonsense poem, it has a lot to say!

ELEMENT THREE:
IRONY AND PARADOX

Poetry like art beautifies the world around us: paintings of beautiful landscapes, the Mona Lisa smile, a poem about a field of daffodils, and the well-chiseled David to name a few. Any type of art that attempts to show the uglier side of people or society is often not popular; it exists for sure, but how many people have a painting of a garbage heap hanging in their living room? Modern poets are known for their portrayal of the everyday, such as T.S. Eliot' s "The Winter Evening Settles Down," which is a beautifully written poem about the ugliness of a modern city street. It could be argued that Eliot's poem is not that ugly of a topic; it is something any urban dweller sees daily, and that is the point. But how many mainstream poems are there on rape, abortion, murder, suicide, and other unsavory topics? Outside of avant-garde publications, these poems do not have an audience, but such topics do, in fact, exist in many poems throughout history; the passive reader just may not notice it at first. Poets are usually the first to bring to press the unsavory or neglected parts of society to light, and they can do it successfully using both irony and paradox.

Irony is manipulating language to express the opposite meaning written often in a humorous fashion. Irony is the perfect form to deal with concepts or ideas that society may be uncomfortable with. Irony is successful as a poetic element because it *is* the truth no matter how unwelcome the idea. When reading irony, a perceptive reader may find it humorous or disturbing, depending on the goal of the poet. The poem may push a wedge between what appears to be the truth and the reality of the truth. For example, in Samuel Taylor Coleridge's "Rhyme of the Ancient Mariner," he deftly uses irony when he writes:

Water, water, every where,
And all the boards did shrink;
Water, water, every where,
Nor any drop to drink.

The appearance of water and the reality of it are two different concepts. A sailor, who has run out of water on the high seas like the Mariner, understands this idea all too well. This is called **situational irony** that contrasts what the reader expects with what really happens. What is expected is that if water is everywhere then it should be drunk, but the situational irony is that it is ocean water, and though it looks refreshing, it cannot be imbibed.

Let's look at how irony is used in another poem. Stephen Crane deals ironically with the theme of disillusionment.

A MAN SAW A BALL OF GOLD

Stephen Crane

A man saw a ball of gold in the sky;
He climbed for it,
And eventually he achieved it --
It was clay.

Now this is the strange part:
When the man went to the earth
And looked again,
Lo, there was a ball of gold.
Now this is the strange part:
It was a ball of gold.
Ay, by the heavens, it was a ball of gold.

The irony is found in line 4 when the "ball of gold" turns out to be nothing but clay! Why is that ironic? Gold is held in high esteem. It is recognized the world over as a precious metal worth achieving, yet when we do achieve it, the ball of gold becomes clay. We may vote for a president who promises to change the status quo of the country only to be elected and become the status quo. The double irony of this poem, though, is that the ball of gold that we have seen as worthless clay is, in reality, a ball of gold. We may buy an item that is clearly valuable, only to find out that after paying the high price, it ceases to have value and becomes just another item we own.

When irony becomes more biting and critical in what it says, it has turned into sarcasm. Jonathan Swift was perhaps one of the best poets to use sarcasm effectively and popularly. In the poem "On Ink", Swift shows the discrepancy between our idea of what ink is and the actual power it has; "the pen is mightier than the sword" indeed.

ON INK

Jonathan Swift (1667-1745)

I am jet black, as you may see,
The son of pitch[20] and gloomy night;
Yet all that know me will agree,
I'm dead except I live in light.

Sometimes in panegyric[21] high,
Like lofty Pindar,[22] I can soar,
And raise a virgin to the sky,
Or sink her to a filthy ----.

My blood this day is very sweet,
To-morrow of a bitter juice;
Like milk, 'tis cried about the street,
And so applied to different use.

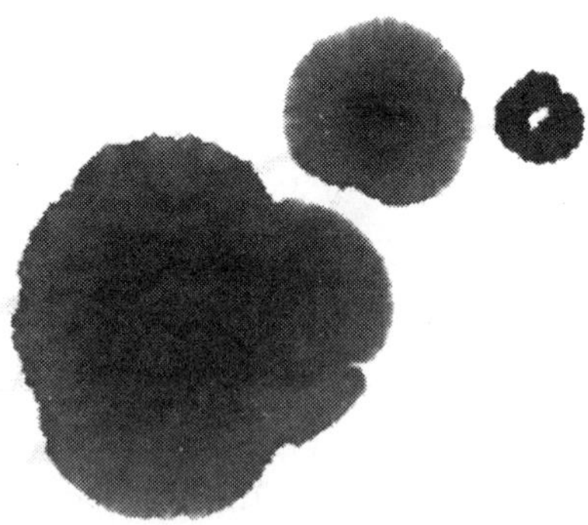

20 pitch: (n) tar

21 panegyric: (n) a lofty praise of a person or thing; eulogy

22 Pindar: ancient Greek poet

Most wondrous is my magic power:
For with one color I can paint;
I'll make the devil a saint this hour,
Next make a devil of a saint.

Through distant regions I can fly,
Provide me but with paper wings;
And fairly show a reason why
There should be quarrels among kings;

And, after all, you'll think it odd,
When learned doctors will dispute,
That I should point the word of God,
And show where they can best confute.

Let lawyers bawl and strain their throats
'Tis I that must the lands convey,
And strip their clients to their coats;
Nay, give their very souls away.

Here we have the personification of ink speaking sarcastically to us, the reader. Swift once wrote in the Preface to *The Battle of the Books* (1704), "Satire is a sort of glass wherein beholders do generally discover everybody' s face but their own." Irony and sarcasm, as a form of satire, are indeed popular because we can see the irony in the lives of others but not in ourselves; thus, we keep reading. "On Ink" does this successfully. All the horrible things we write and profess with pen and ink are dumped on the "scapegoat" ink. Because ink is personified, it becomes the villain, not the person who writes with it. The sarcasm of this poem can be restated in another modern form, "Guns don't kill people, bullets do." This phrase shifts the blame from the gun that is seen as violent to something else entirely—the bullets, and yet it has an essence of truth. But what is missing is the reality behind the quote, that being, "Guns don't kill people, people do."

"On Ink" is performing a similar function, albeit 400 years earlier. By focusing on the evils that we commit in the written form, the poem allows us to force the blame onto others—lawyers, politicians, writers. We fail to see that the poem implicates us in this negative action, which is why we are drawn to it, but it does raise the issue of the damage the written word causes society without making anyone angry.

Paradox is another popular element in poems. What may at first seem contradictory starts to make sense upon a second or third reading. It is similar to irony in that they both are aware of illusion and reality, and what we read must not always be taken at face value. A common modern paradox is that we drive our car to a trendy health club, take the elevator up to the tenth floor, then get on the stair machine. To someone who is not a modern, this appears as a paradox, to the rest of us we can understand why it can be a paradox but understand why it is so. Just running up stairs is not the main source of exercise; we want to feel connected to others by being part of a "group" or established "product." For a sense of paradox, let's look at the first stanza of John Keats's "Ode to a Nightingale."

ODE TO A NIGHTINGALE

John Keats

My heart aches, and a drowsy numbness pains
My sense, as though of hemlock[23] I had drunk,
Or emptied some dull opiate to the drains[24]
One minute past, and Lethe-wards[25] had sunk:
'Tis not through envy of thy happy lot,
But being too happy in thine happiness,—
That thou, light-winged Dryad[26] of the trees,
In some melodious plot
Of beechen[27] green, and shadows numberless,
Singest of summer in full-throated ease.

23 hemlock: (n) a poisonous drink

24 drain: (n) meaning something that has drained away

25 Lethe-wards: towards Lethe, a mythical river in Hades where the dead drank to forget the past

26 Dryad: nymphs that live in forests

27 beechen: (adj) of relating to a beech tree

This first stanza introduces the nightingale as being "too happy in thine happiness." Viewing such happiness causes the speaker to feel bouts of both pain and joy. The paradox is expressed when the speaker states in the first line that his heart aches while being overcome with drowsy numbness. On first reading, we may wonder how the speaker can ache and be numb all at once. Such a paradox creates a shocking image of pain of how the speaker feels hearing the voice of a nightingale. This contradictory phrasing is known as an **oxymoron**, which lies at the center of many paradoxes. When the speaker says, "drowsy numbness pains," he is speaking of a pain that is so intense that he cannot deal with it so that the pain finally numbs his senses. This is how the speaker can paradoxically feel a numbness that can cause pain. We can take away from this paradox that the speaker knows he will never be like the nightingale, free from the pains of the world.

Another type of paradox is found in religious poetry, the idea that fallen, imperfect humans can somehow follow and obey an exalted, perfect God. Nobody experienced the paradox of religion more than George Herbert, a church minister who found it difficult to call a congregation of sinners to repentance while he himself was also a sinner, for ministers are human, and, therefore, sin. This paradox is wonderfully expressed in "The Collar."

THE COLLAR

George Herbert (1593-1633)

I struck the board,[28] and cried, No more;
I will abroad.
What? shall I ever sigh and pine?[29]
My lines and life are free; free as the road,
Loose as the wind, as large as store.[30]
Shall I be still in suit?[31]
Have I no harvest but a thorn
To let me blood, and not restore
What I have lost with cordial[32] fruit?
Sure there was wine,
Before my sighs did dry it: there was corn
Before my tears did drown it.
Is the year only lost to me?
Have I no bays[33] to crown it?
No flowers, no garlands gay? all blasted?
All wasted?
Not so, my heart: but there is fruit,
And thou hast hands.
Recover all thy sigh-blown age
On double pleasures: leave thy cold dispute
Of what is fit, and not forsake thy cage,
Thy rope of sands,[34]

28 board: (n) table

29 pine: (v) regret or yearn

30 store: (n) abundance

31 suit: (adj) asking favors

32 cordial: (adj) life-giving

33 bay: (n) a wreath of leaves; a laurel worn by poets

34 rope of sands: Christian limitations on conduct (rope weak like sand) that is changed into "good cable"

Which petty thoughts have made, and made to thee
Good cable, to enforce and draw,
And be thy law,
While thou didst wink and wouldst not see.
Away; take heed:
I will abroad.
Call in thy deaths-head[35] there: tie up thy fears.
He that forbears
To suit and serve his need,
Deserves his load.
But as I raved and grew more fierce and wild,
At every word,
Me thought I heard one calling, *Child*:
And I replied, *My Lord*.

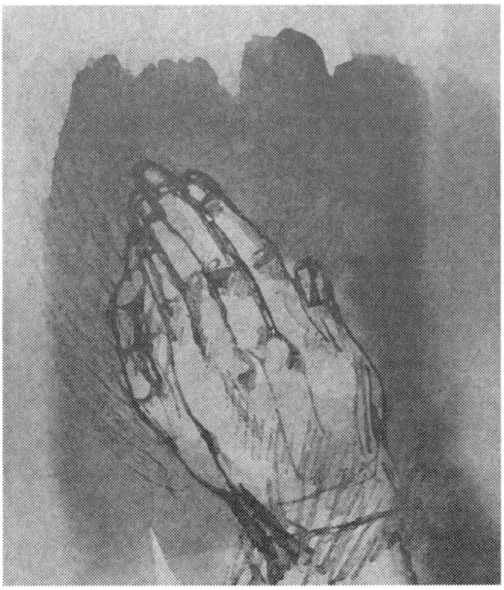

35 deaths-head: (n) a skull; symbolizing mortality

Here, the speaker, also a minister, strikes the table board set with meat and fruit. It appears that he was in the midst of prayer and ends it by striking the table and says he will leave his life of ministry ("I will abroad"). He complains that God has given him nothing but misery for faithful service, a thorn instead of fruit. The corn and wine of the sacrament he sees only as temporal rewards—he has forgotten the eternal significance of these emblems. He plans on a life of pleasure before he is too old. He calls his service to God a cage and God's law as shackles. While he raves and grows "more fierce and wild," he hears the still, small voice of God call out, "Child!" He responds, "My Lord."

The paradox is that a sinner by the very nature of the word is a person who is in opposition to the laws of God. Furthermore, the speaker feels this very paradox even more so as a minister and wishes to leave a spiritual life behind. Yet, when God calls out to him, he is more than willing to respond and continue on.

The paradox is further explored in the very nature of the title itself. The collar means both the collar of a priest and a contraption that restrains an unruly animal (a sinner perhaps?). The third symbol invoked is the play on words with the homophone "caller". The caller, of course, being God at the end of the poem.

ELEMENT FOUR: FIGURES OF SPEECH

Language is full of figurative language. When a friend says, "I didn't mean to say that. It was a slip of the tongue," he doesn't literally mean his tongue has slipped in his mouth, for how is that possible? We understand that he has said something by accident. The English language is full of such figurative language, or figures of speech, and poetry exercises it the best. There are over 250 different forms of figures of speech. We will focus on the four basic and most popular forms.

The first form is the **metaphor** where one object is identified with another and the first object takes on the characteristics of the second. If a picture is worth a thousand words, so then is a metaphor. I could say that John is a tiger. Do I mean that there is a tiger named John? Not likely. What I mean is that John takes on the characteristics of a tiger. Instead of going through a shopping list of attributes about John's temperamental and feisty nature, I can just paint a picture in the mind using a metaphor. We now know that when we are around John, we should be careful of his temper, lest he lashes out. A vivid example of metaphor is found in Andrew Marvell's "To His Coy Mistress," where he writes, "Time's winged chariot hurrying near." Now we know that time does not ride a chariot nor do chariots fly. Thus, the metaphor conjures images of the god Apollo riding his chariot through the heavens, while creating the image of time being fast and always on the move, being immortal.

Traditionally, metaphors were the staple of poets, though they are used much more conservatively in modern times. While most poets restrict metaphors to single instances, classical poets often employed the **extended metaphor** where the metaphorical symbol is developed beyond the single word. For example, Walt Whitman's "O Captain! My Captain!" is a fitting eulogy written after the assassination of Abraham Lincoln.

O CAPTAIN! MY CAPTAIN!

Walt Whitman (1819-1892)

O Captain! my Captain! our fearful trip is done,
The ship has weathered every rack[36], the prize we sought is won,
The port is near, the bells I hear, the people all exulting[37],
While follow eyes the steady keel[38], the vessel grim and daring;
But O heart! heart! heart!
O the bleeding drops of red,
Where on the deck my Captain lies,
Fallen cold and dead.

O Captain! my Captain! rise up and hear the bells;
Rise up—for you the flag is flung for you the bugle trills[39],

36 rack: (n) violent twist

37 exulting: (v) rejoicing

38 keel: (n) often referred to as a ship in literature

39 trill: (v) to call out

For you bouquets and ribbon'd wreaths—for you the shores a-crowding,
For you they call, the swaying mass, their eager faces turning;
Here Captain! dear father!
This arm beneath your head!
It is some dream that on the deck,
You've fallen cold and dead.

My Captain does not answer, his lips are pale and still;
My father does not feel my arm, he has no pulse nor will;
The ship is anchored safe and sound, its voyage closed and done;
From fearful trip the victor ship comes in with object won;
Exult O shores, and ring O bells!
But I, with mournful tread,
Walk the deck my Captain lies,
Fallen cold and dead.

O Captain! my Captain, our fearful trip is done,
The ship has weathered every rack, the prize we sought is won,
The port is near, the bells I hear, the people all exulting,
While follow eyes the steady keel, the vessel grim and daring;
But O heart! heart! heart!
O the bleeding drips of red,
Where on the deck my Captain lies,
Fallen cold and dead.

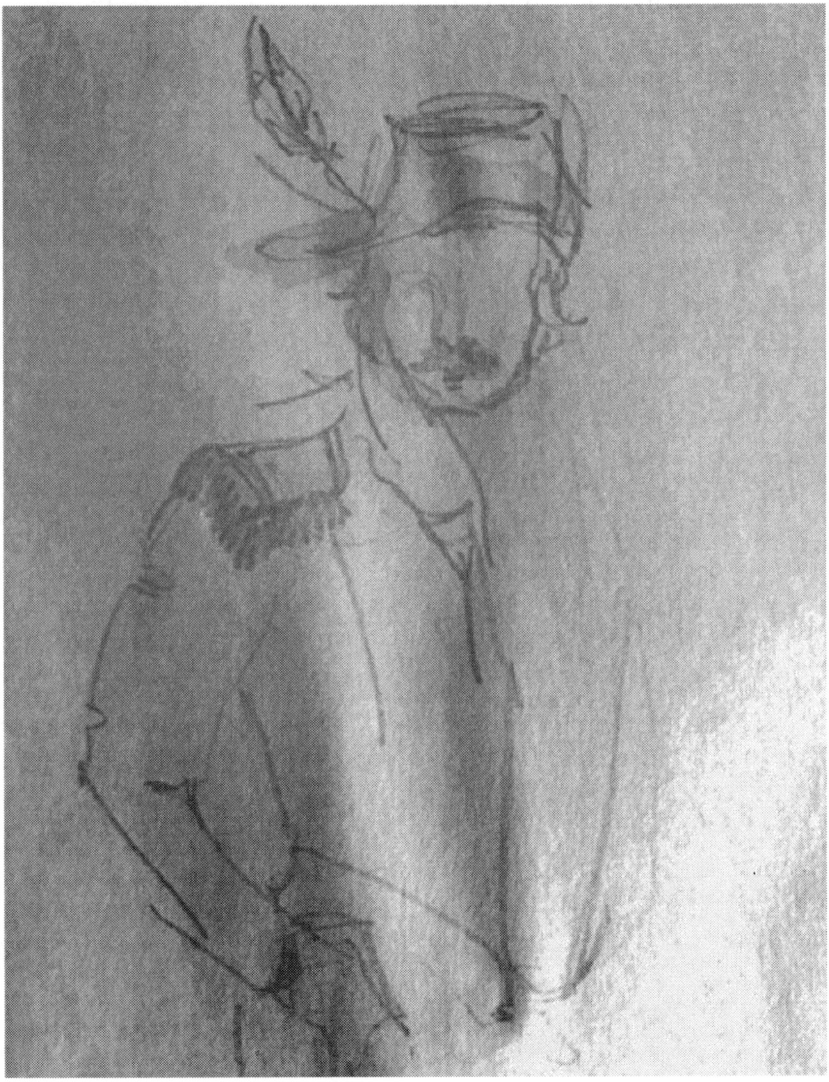

Utilizing **apostrophe**, a figure of speech where the narrator directly speaks to someone not present, Whitman gives adoration to Lincoln, whose death shocked the nation. Whitman spoke about how he had a dream of a ship under full sail entering the harbor the night before Lincoln was shot. Whitman couples the ship entering port metaphor with President Lincoln as the captain of the ship, which represents the newly won Union of the American states. Lincoln, as the captain, has survived the tumultuous storm (The Civil War) that almost destroyed his vessel (America). Just as he nears the port (the end of the war), he is received as a hero; but, to the dismay of those waiting, he has "fallen cold and dead" on the deck of his ship.

The second stanza is the narrator's wish the death of such a great man, who turns out to be his father, is only a dream as he holds the captain in his arms. The third stanza reaffirms it is not a dream, but the death of the captain was not in vain. Though the ship has come to port with the leader now passed on, the goal of the ship returning safely has been accomplished. Whitman's tone and use of words such as "fallen cold and dead" deepen the tragedy of death for such a revered person, but there is also hope in the poem as well, for no matter how we die, it is how we live our life that is of utmost importance.

Another type of figure of speech is related to the metaphor—**personification**, or giving human characteristics to animals, inanimate objects, or natural occurrences. Take, for example, the following sonnet.

HOLY SONNET 10

John Donne

Death be not proud, though some have called thee
Mighty and dreadful, for thou are not so;
For those whom thou thinkst, thou does overthrow
Die not, poor death, nor yet canst thou kill me.
From rest and sleep, which but they pictures be,
Much pleasure—then from thee much more must flow,
And soonest our best men with thee do go,
Rest of their bones, and soul's delivery.
Thou art slave to fate, chance, kings, and desperate men,
And dost with poison, war, and sickness dwell,
And poppy or charms can make us sleep as well,
And better then thy stroke; why swellst thou then?
One short sleep past, we wake eternally
And death shall be no more; Death, thou shalt die.

Here, Death is personified as a real person. By doing so, the poet can tap into a vast vault of symbolism, knowing the reader will understand the figurative language being used. In literature, Death is often a figure to be feared, and, as in John Milton's *Paradise Lost*, Death is even greater than Satan while having the power to even harm him. Donne only scoffs at that image. His sonnet explains the absolute powerlessness Death has over us. We all die, but it is a gate to a greater place. This horrible apparition that is Death is merely a slave of "fate, chance, kings, and desperate men" who are the ones that decide who will live or die, and not Death himself. Death's only companions, it turns out, are "poison, war, and sickness," but we can imitate death with certain drugs (the poppy) and charms (hypnotism), so what is so special about what Death does? While we go on to live for eternity through Christ' s resurrection, Death will eventually end, and he, not we, shall die. Now try writing a poem on such a topic without invoking figures of speech. It would be nearly impossible.

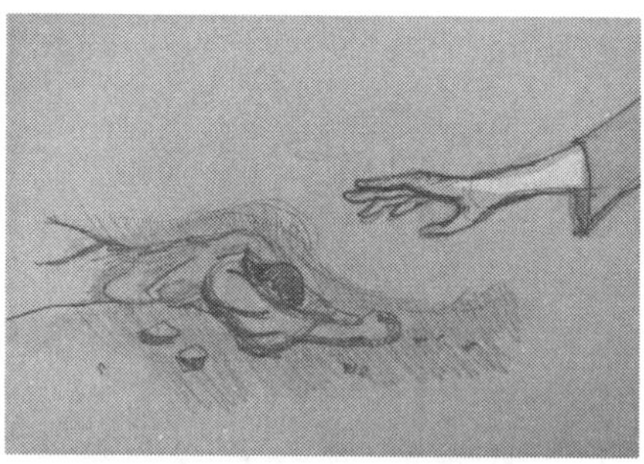

A third common type of figure of speech is the **simile**. Where a metaphor simply states one idea for another, a simile uses comparison through the words *like* or *as*. To make a distinction between a metaphor and a simile, let's look at "A Red, Red Rose" by Robert Burns.

A RED, RED ROSE

Robert Burns

O my Luve is like a red, red rose
That's newly sprung in June;
O my Luve is like the melody
That's sweetly played in tune.

So fair art thou, my bonnie lass[40],
So deep in luve am I;
And I will luve thee still, my dear,
Till a' the seas gang dry[41].

Till a' the seas gang dry, my dear,
And the rocks melt wi' the sun;
I will love thee still, my dear,
While the sands o' life shall run.

And fare thee weel, my only luve!
And fare thee weel awhile!
And I will come again, my luve,
Though it were ten thousand mile.

40 bonnie lass: (n) Scottish for pretty girl

41 gang dry: Scottish for "go dry"

The first two lines of the poem form a simile. "O my luve's like a red, red rose / That's newly sprung in June." His love is *like* a red rose is an approximation. It is like saying in a mathematical formula Love ≈ Red Rose. If the poet had wanted to use metaphor, he would have phrased it this way: "O my love is a red, red rose." As a metaphor, his love takes on the characteristics of the red rose; they are both equal in meaning. Thus, the associations that the sentence brings to the meaning are broader than the simile. The mathematical formula would be Love = Red Rose. The simile only stipulates that his love is like a red rose, so the comparison is limited in its approximation. The metaphor can literally have every single quality that a red rose may possess, including all the connotations. We can understand how far the poet wants us to take the symbolism used. With similes, we are restricted; with metaphors, we are freer in our interpretations.

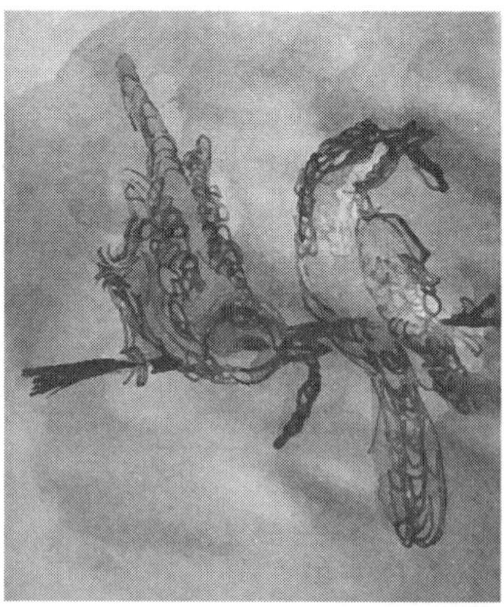

Do not confuse the **hyperbole**, another figure of speech, with a simile. Hyperboles are often written as similes, as in the man is as tall as a mountain, except the only function this statement has is to exaggerate the concept of how tall the man is. A hyperbole, Greek for "excess," is often used poetically as an extreme form of exaggeration, where poets wish to highlight atypical and expressive imagery. Sylvia Plath exercises hyperbole in "Daddy" to express how much influence she feels her father has held over her. "Daddy, I have to kill you. / You died before I had time--- / Marble-heavy, a bag full of gold, / Ghastly statue with one gray toe / Big as a Frisco seal / And a head in the freakish Atlantic." Here Plath expresses both metaphor and hyperbole to detail her own feeling about her father's influence over her as being so overwhelming and grand that his control is a colossal statue stretched from the Atlantic Ocean in the west all the way to San Francisco (Frisco) in the east. The toe of this metaphorical statue is the size of a San Francisco seal that is well known for its large size, which is also expressed as a hyperbole.

Another hyperbole that does not use comparison is just gross exaggeration, as found in "The Concord Hymn" by Ralph Waldo Emerson.

CONCORD HYMN

Ralph Waldo Emerson (1803-1882)

Sung at the Completion of the Battle Monument, July 4, 1837

By the rude bridge that arched the flood,
Their flag to April's breeze unfurled,
Here once the embattled farmers stood
And fired the shot heard round the world.

The foe long since in silence slept;
Alike the conqueror silent sleeps;
And Time the ruined bridge has swept
Down the dark stream which seaward creeps.

On this green bank, by this soft stream,
We set today a votive stone;
That memory may their deed redeem,
When, like our sires, our sons are gone.

Spirit, that made those heroes dare
To die, and leave their children free,
Bid Time and Nature gently spare
The shaft we raise to them and thee.

Emerson wrote this poem in commemoration of the first battle of the American Revolution. He writes, “Here once the embattled farmers stood; / And fired the shot heard round the world.” We can see the revolutionaries first shot that started the war could literally not have been heard around the world, but the idea that the effect of this shot, would have repercussions that would be felt around the world, namely the spread of freedom and democracy around the globe. Thus, the use of hyperbole for effect.

ELEMENT FIVE: THE SOUND OF POETRY

Poetry has a distinct sound that separates it from prose. We often think of poetry as rhyming, and, indeed, most of the classical forms of poetry do rhyme as are found in this anthology; however, the modern movement of the early 20th century moved poetry into non-rhyming verse, which has various forms, such as **free verse** and blank verse. Without rhyme, poets rely on other techniques, such as syntax, to give shape to their poems. Consider the free verse poem "The Young Housewife".

THE YOUNG HOUSE WIFE

William Carlos Williams

At ten A.M. the young housewife
moves about in negligee[42] behind
the wooden walls of her husband's house.
I pass solitary in my car.

Then again she comes to the curb
to call the ice-man, fish-man, and stands
shy, uncorseted,[43] tucking in
stray ends of hair, and I compare her
to a fallen leaf.

The noiseless wheels of my car
rush with a crackling sound over
dried leaves as I bow and pass smiling.

42 negligee: (n) a light, revealing nightgown

43 uncorseted: a corset is a tight-fitting garment meant to make a woman look slim; it connotes being under male control; being uncorseted suggests being free of her husband's influence

True **free verse** strays as far from tradition as possible by creating imagery and emotion instead of strict poetic formulas. In the above poem, the poet is "painting" a picture of a lonely housewife by avoiding traditional techniques of rhyme, rhythm, and meter. Notice that the poem utilizes syntax to create poetic form instead of rhyme. Instead of the standard layout to create rhythm, Williams creates his own pauses by creating short stanzas and lines. If we look at the third line in the second stanza we can see the effect of non-traditional line breaking. The young housewife goes to the curb to talk to different deliverymen, being shy and uncorseted. When the speaker mentions her "tucking in" something, we automatically assume she is going to tuck in an article of clothing, but the next line reveals it is her hair. We now realize that she is more concerned about her looks than we were led to believe.

Let's now look at another example of free verse by Robert Frost.

MENDING WALL

Robert Frost

Something there is that doesn't love a wall,
That sends the frozen-ground-swell under it,
And spills the upper boulders in the sun,
And makes gaps even two can pass abreast.
The work of hunters is another thing:
I have come after them and made repair
Where they have left not one stone on a stone,
But they would have the rabbit out of hiding,
To please the yelping dogs. The gaps I mean,
No one has seen them made or heard them made,
But at spring mending-time we find them there.

The lines do not rhyme, but they do still maintain a regular structure of iambic pentameter, which also requires ten syllables per line for the most part. Line 8 does have eleven syllables to force the rhythm to stumble, thus, forcing the reader to pay extra attention to what is being said, which is highlighted in the following line by putting a period in the middle, creating **caesura**. Free verse has been as popular as rhyming poetry in that most epic poetry and plays utilize it. For example, John Milton's *Paradise Lost* and most of Shakespeare's plays have free verse.

Rhymed poetry, however, is so much more difficult to produce than most readers think. In fact, Robert Frost visited students at Milton Academy in 1935 and said, "I had soon write free verse as play tennis with the net down."[44] There is some truth to this statement. Rhyming adds an element of challenge, but it adds a whole new dimension to understanding the poem. Poets not only have to match the final consonant and vowel sounds of two or more words, they have to decide where to place the corresponding rhymes. When the same ending sounds occur at the end of lines, they are called **end rhymes**, and when they are found within the lines, they are called **internal rhymes**.

End rhymes are easy to find and are the most popular.

44 Robert Frost: Collected Poems, Prose, and Plays. Library of America, page 809

UPON JULIA'S CLOTHES

Robert Herrick

Whenas[45] in silks my Julia g*oes*,
Then, then, methinks, how sweetly fl*ows*
That liquefaction[46] of her cl*othes*.

Next, when I cast mine eyes, and s*ee*
That brave vibration, each way fr*ee*,
O, how that glittering taketh m*e*!

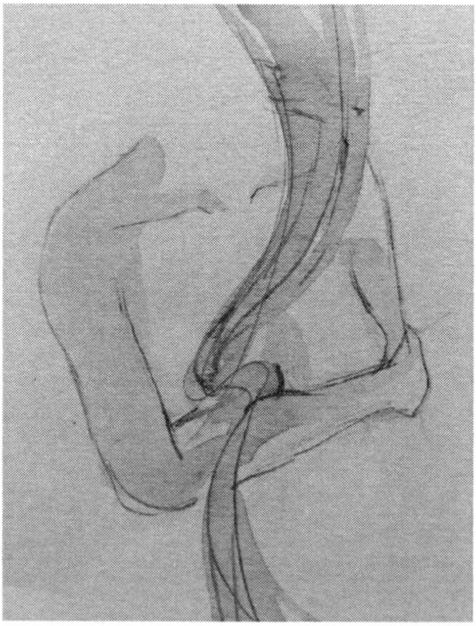

45 whenas: (conj) old form meaning 'when'

46 liquefaction: (n) the state of being liquid or looking like liquid

Each stanza has three end rhymes that are exact—*goes*, *flows*, *clothes*, for example. Such rhymes create an allusion of repetition without boring the reader. End rhymes are also excellent for giving closure to a poem, giving closure to the reading experience. This is especially used well in the **closed couplet**. Shakespeare used the couplet with utmost satisfaction in his sonnets, as in "So long as men can breathe, or eyes can s*ee*, / So long lives this, and this gives life to th*ee*" found at the end of "Sonnet 18".

Internal rhyme is another devise that is common in poetry but may not be noticed as much by first time readers. One of the best poems to use internal rhyme is "The Raven" by Edgar Allan Poe.

Once upon a midnight **dreary**, while I pondered, weak and **weary**,
Over many a quaint and curious volume of forgotten *lore*,
While I noded, nearly **napping**, suddenly
there came a **tapping**,
As of someone gently **rapping, rapping** at my chamber *door*.
"'Tis some visitor," I muttered, "**tapping** at my chamber *door* —
Only this, and nothing *more*."

The bolded words indicate the internal rhyme, while the italicized words are the end rhymes. What makes Poe's poem even more memorable is that he was able to use both end and internal rhyme to his advantage.

Rhymes are not as straightforward as we may originally think. As you may have noticed, not all rhymes sound perfectly the same, or even have the same stress. There are several forms of general rhymes that we should know before we proceed: alliteration, assonance, consonance, half rhyme, masculine and feminine rhymes, sight rhyme, slant rhyme, and triple rhyme.

First, **alliteration** is matching the first consonants of words and can be found throughout a line. Most popular with Old English poetry, it survives to this day. An example is found in Poe's "The Raven" when he writes, "weak and weary", "quaint and curious", and "While I nodded, nearly napping."

Another rhyme is **assonance**, where the vowels are matched instead of the consonants, as in Alfred Lord Tennyson's "The Lotus-Eaters."

> **A**nd round **a**bout the keel[47] with f*a*ces p*a*le,
> Dark f*a*ces p*a*le ag*ai*nst that rosy fl*a*me,
> The m**i**ld-**eye**d melancholy Lotos-eaters c*a*me.

Assonance is achieved with the long "a" sound in all three lines. There is also assonance found in the short "a" sound in the first line and the long "i" in the third line.

Next, we have **consonance**, which matches any consonants in the line as opposed to just the initial consonants of alliteration. Further into Poe's "The Raven" consonance is beautifully written, "And the **s**ilken **s**ad un**c**ertain

47 keel: (n) boat or ship

ru**s**tling of each p*ur*ple c*ur*tain." Notice the assonance of the "ur" sound at the end of the line as well.

The fourth type usually created as the result of consonance is the **half** (or sprung) **rhyme**, where the final consonants are matched at the end of the lines, but the vowels do not. William Butler Yeats wrote many of his poems in half rhyme as the following poem illustrates.

LINES WRITTEN IN DEJECTION

William Butler Yeats

When have I last looked o*n*
The round green eyes and the long wavering bodies
Of the dark leopards of the moo*n*?
All the wild witches, those most noble ladies,
For all their broom-sticks and their tears,
Their angry tears, are go*n*e.
The holy centaurs[48] of the hills are vanished;
I have nothing but the embittered su*n*;
Banished heroic mother moon and vanished,
And now that I have come to fifty years
I must endure the timid su*n*.

48 centaur: (n) a mythical creature with the upper body of a man and lower body of a horse

Notice that "on" and "moon" both end with the same vowel and consonant, but the vowels are different—short vowel and long vowel. "Gone" and "sun" have different vowels, but the same consonant ending while the other lines have the more traditional end rhyme usage.

A **masculine rhyme**, or single rhyme, has the two or more words that rhyme through the final syllables, which are stressed, or which are only one syllable. Most of the rhymes in this book are masculine rhymes, as can be seen from the first part of John Donne's "Lecture Upon a Shadow."

Stand still, and I will read to *thee*
A lecture, love, in Love's philoso*phy*.
    These three hours that we have *spent*
    Walking here, two shadows *went*
Along with us, which we ourselves pro*duced*.
But now the sun is just above our *head*,
    We do those shadows *tread*,
    And to brave clearness all things are re*duced*.

A **feminine rhyme** has two syllables that rhyme; therefore, is also known as a double rhyme. The first syllable is stressed with an unstressed consonant. Robert Frost loved to write with both masculine and feminine rhymes.

NOTHING GOLD CAN STAY

Robert Frost

Nature's first green is g*old*,
Her hardest hue to h*old*.
Her early leaf's a fl*ower*;
But only so an h*our*.
Then leaf subsides to l*eaf*.
So Eden[49] sank to gr*ief*,
So dawn goes down to d*ay*.
Nothing gold can st*ay*.

49 Eden: the Biblical paradise where the first man and woman, Adam and Eve, were created and were later cast out of for eating the forbidden fruit

Notice that the last syllables in bold are masculine rhymes while "flower" and "hour," with two rhyming syllables are feminine. You may have noticed that "today" is split into two words, "to day." This is not a typing error; it is to maintain his masculine rhyme scheme."

Frost also used feminine rhyme to call attention to certain words or ideas. This is made obvious in the last stanza of his poem "Reluctance," where he interspersed feminine rhymes with masculine endings:

> Ah, when to the heart of man
> Was it ever less than a tr*eason*
> To go with the drift of things,
> To yield with a grace to r*eason*,
> And bow and accept the end
> Of a love or a s*eason*?

Notice the bold words are feminine rhymes following masculine ending lines. If we look closely at the last stanza, Frost purposefully accented "season" on the second to last syllable so that it would be a feminine rhyme. Feminine rhymes are more difficult to use than masculine rhymes. How many words rhyme with season? Frost would take words like "treason" and "reason" just to use them for their feminine rhyme, and then separate them with masculine endings that didn't rhyme but had one syllable. Notice that he offsets the feminine rhyme lines to accentuate the difference between his masculine ending and feminine rhyme.

A seventh type of rhyme **sight rhymes** cause some confusion for second language learners because they have the same spelling, but the pronunciation is a little off or completely different. A good example of a sight rhyme is found in the second stanza of "The Snail" by William Cowper.

Wherever he dwells, he dwells al**one**,
Except himself, has chattels[50] n**one**,
Well satisfied to be his own
        Whole treasure.

Though the spelling of the final syllables is the same in the first two lines, "alone" has a long vowel, whereas "none" has a short vowel. These should not be forced to rhyme but pronounced as is. Robert Herrick used imperfect rhymes frequently in his poetry such as in "His Return to London." "Ravished in spirit, I come, nay more I fl*y* / To thee, blest place of my nativit*y*!" Again, do not force the rhyme, but let it be pronounced as is natural.

Eighth, **slant rhymes** are forms of half rhymes, and are important to know. They are created through either assonance or consonance, which creates a sound close enough to another's, but it is still not quite a full rhyme. Let's look at Dickinson's poem "The Difference Between Despair" for a good example of a slant rhyme:

The Mind is Smooth—no Motion—
Contented as the E*ye*
Upon the Forehead of a Bust—
That knows—it cannot s*ee*.

"Eye" and "see" do not perfectly rhyme, but they do create a slant rhyme through the similarity of end vowels. Such a rhyme is evocative, even disconcerting; the slant on the rhyme matches the slant on the theme. The eye on the "forehead

50 chattel: (n) belongings

of a bust" that Dickenson mentions could reference a statue of a Cyclops, whose sight is already hindered by having just one eye. The tragedy of the final two lines is that its hindered sight is completely blinded as a statue.

The final type, a **triple rhyme**, is where two words with a stressed syllable are followed by two unstressed syllables that rhyme. Lord Byron used triple rhyme rather well throughout his long satirical poem *Don Juan.* A good example as any is found in stanza 20 of Canto One:

Now Donna[51] Inez had, with all her m*erit*,
    A great opinion of her own good qualities;
Neglect, indeed, requires a saint to b*ear it*,
    And such, indeed, she was in her moralities;
But then she had a devil of a sp*irit*,
    And sometimes mixed up fancies with realities,
And let few opportunities escape
    Of getting her liege lord into a scrape.

As can be imagined, to get these three triple rhymes, Byron had to choose them before he wrote the verse and then match up his ideas to fit. Notice the feminine rhymes in *italics*. With an understanding of the different types of rhyme, we can get a better appreciation as to how difficult it can be to construct a poem of absolute beauty.

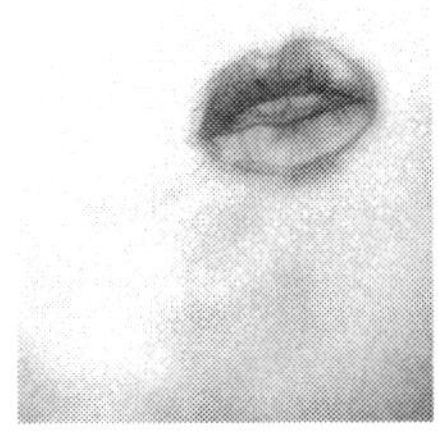

Let's now take a final look at a poem by Gerard Manley Hopkins that incorporates as many of our rhymes as possible. I have marked them where used.

51 donna: a Spanish title equivalent to Mrs.; don is equivalent to Mr.

SPRING AND FALL: TO A YOUNG CHILD

Gerard Manley Hopkins

Márgáret, are you griéving   assonance
Over Goldengrove[52] unleaving?
Leaves, **l**ike the things of man, you   **alliteration**
With your **f**resh thoughts care **f**or, can you?
Ah! as the heart grows older
It will come to such sights colder[53]   feminine rhymes
By and **b**y, nor **s**pare a **s**igh   masculine rhymes
Though **w**orlds of **w**anwood[54] leafmeal[55] lie;
And yet you **w**ill **w**eep and know **w**hy.
Now no matter, child, the name:
Sorrow's **s**prings are the same.   consonance
Nor **m**outh had, no nor **m**ind, expressed
What **h**éart **h**éard of, **g**hóst **g**uéssed:
It is the **b**light **m**an was **b**orn for,
It is **M**argaret you **m**ourn for.

52 Golden Grove: an Elizabethan period manor that was prominent in Hopkins's time

53 colder: in this case meaning 'less emotion'

54 wanwood: probably meaning 'a dark forest'

55 leafmeal: another form meaning "piecemeal'; all the leaves of the forest have fallen

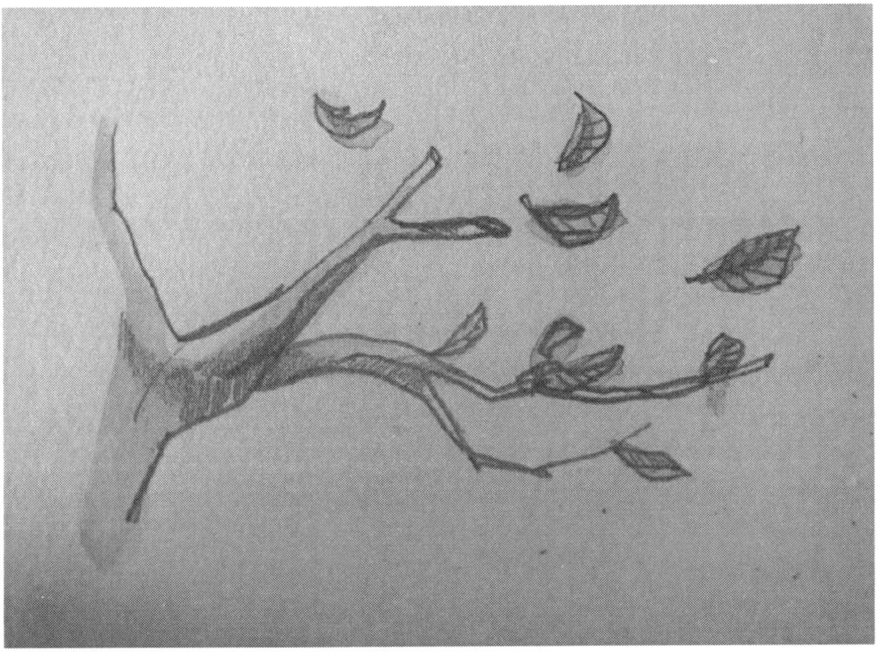

Because every line rhymes, every ending syllable is considered an ending rhyme. Hopkins does use an *internal rhyme* in line 7 when he writes, "By and b*y*, nor spare a s*igh*."

Glossary

Alliteration: the repetition of the opening consonant sounds or any vowel sounds in adjacent words.

Apostrophe: a figure of speech where the narrator directly speaks to someone not present.

Assonance: a type of alliteration where the vowels of adjacent words rhyme while the end consonants are different. Not to be confused with a rhyme. A rhyme is "fight" and "right". Assonance is "cake" and "lake".

Autobiographical "I": the rare occasion when the speaker of a poem and the poet are the same person.

Big Six: the six main poets of the Romantic period, respectively William Wordsworth, Samuel Taylor Coleridge, Lord George Gordon Byron, Percy Shelley, and John Keats.

Byronic Hero: a character often found in Lord Byron's poetry who often rebels and then suffers exile, while his talent and passions help bring about self-destruction.

Caesura: a break in the middle of a poetic line to stop the regular flow of the verse.

Closed Couplet: two successive lines with the same end rhyme. It must contain a complete grammatical sentence and usually ends a sonnet.

Compound-Complex Sentence: a sentence containing at least one dependent clause and two dependent clauses.

Conceit: a type of poetic metaphor that expresses an idea through an elaborate analogy where one idea is connected to a dissimilar idea and expounded on. A common conceit is comparing love to a rose.

Concrete Images: words or phrases that stimulate the senses directly as if the reader were there to witness the scene.

Connotation: the emotional idea or attitude of the word.

Consonance: a type of alliteration where the consonants in two words rhyme but the vowels do not, such as "tor<u>n</u>" and "bur<u>n</u>".

Denotation: the meaning of a word as found in a dictionary, empty of any emotions or attitudes.

Diction: a style of language that stands out from the common usage and is reliant on word choice.

Dramatic Monologue: a poem written like a speech in a play, given by an individual character.

Elegy: a thoughtful formal poem that laments the dead.

Ellipsis: a type of poetic syntax when the poet leaves words out of sentences where the reader usually expects to read them.

End Rhyme: the same ending sounds occurring at the end of lines.

Epic: a lengthy poem narrating the lofty actions of heroes and gods.

Epigram: short, balanced, and elegant sayings made popular during ancient Greece by Martial (40-104) and popularized in the English language by Ben Jonson.

Epiphany: an enlightening revelation suddenly perceived in a quick flash of recognition. An everyday idea or object is thus seen in a new light.

Extended Metaphor: the metaphorical symbol is developed beyond the single word to incorporate an idea that extends throughout the story.

Feminine Rhyme: two syllables that rhyme in corresponding words. Also known as a double rhyme.

Figures of Speech: figurative form of expression used to give meaning through relating one thing or idea with another that has a familiar meaning to the reader.

Free Verse: a type of poetry that strays as far from tradition as possible by creating imagery and emotion instead of strict poetic formulas.

Hyperbole: an excessive exaggeration used for literary effect.

Iambic Pentameter: a line with ten syllables with the first syllable stressed and the second unstressed. Iamb means two, and pentameter means five. In other words, two types of stresses in five metrical feet.

Imagery: an assortment of images in a poem. As a figure of speech, the basic meanings of a word are changed for poetic style.

Internal Rhyme: the same ending sounds found within the same line.

Irony: the manipulation of language to express the opposite meaning, sometimes written in a humorous fashion.

Masculine Rhyme: two or more words that rhyme through the final syllables, which are stressed, or which are only one syllable. Also known as a single rhyme.

Metaphor: one object is identified with another and the first object takes on the characteristics of the second for easy understanding.

Metaphysical Conceit: a paradoxical, complex, and often shocking comparison of one idea with another.

Objective Correlative: the arousing of the reader's emotions through a pattern of objects, actions, or events without relying on a "formula" of those responses, formulated by T.S. Eliot.

Octave: a verse form containing eight lines.

Oxymoron: from the Greek meaning "sharp-dull." A combination or words with contradictory meaning to create an effect, such as "numbing pain" "tears of joy."

Paradox: a statement that seems contradictory but upon closer thought, may actually be true.

Personification: giving human characteristics to animals, inanimate objects, or natural occurrences.

Poetry of Sensibility: an expression of spontaneous feelings of the heart to express truth in place of reason and law set forth by a male-dominated society.

Pun: a play on words where the similarity in sound between two words with different meanings are used for comedic effect, as in the famous Shakespearean pun, "Now is the **winter** or our discontent made glorious **summer** by this **sun** of York." Sun instead of son is the pun.

Quaker: a dissenting Christian sect that broke away from the Church of England in the 18th century who believed God resides in everyone. Popular with women, it taught universal priesthood (both men and women could be priests). The name derived from the way the followers "quake" before for the lord.

Sarcasm: similar to irony but harsher and nastier, usually used in a personal, mocking way in order to cause harm.

Sestet: the second, six-line division of an Italian sonnet. Sestets usually follow the eight-line division, an octet, and make a statement about the theme set up in the octet.

Sibilance: the creation of strongly stressed consonants by forcing air from the throat through the lips and tongue.

Simile: comparing two objects and likening one object to another through the words "as" or "like". It is more indirect than a metaphor.

Situational Irony: a type of irony where the poet contrasts what the reader expects with what really happens, as in lover's quarreling, or a whale drowning.

Slant Rhymes: a half rhyme where the assonance or consonance are replaced for a true rhyme as in "tongue" and "from" or "lover" and "over".

Syntax: how the words are arranged in any given sentence and the rules governing their arrangement.

Triple Rhyme: two words with a stressed syllable followed by two unstressed syllables that rhyme.

Volta: an unexpected or surprising thematic twist—usually from a question to an answer or a problem to a solution—that begins the sestet in an Italian sonnet.

Word Play: a poetic device that uses words specifically as the main subject in the entire poem. Donne's "The Flea" is a good example of word play, playfully referencing the mixing of blood in a flea to sexual union and the killing of the flea to murder. Puns, rhetorical questions, obscure words and unusual meanings are all types of word play.

INDEX OF FIRST LINES

INDEX OF AUTHORS & TITLES

INDEX OF FIFTY RECITED POEMS

Read by Steven Reeder
Recorded at Dongseo University Studio
Edited by Oksun Kang

INDEX

F

G

H

I

J

K

L

M

N

O

P

Q

R

S

T

U

V

W

Y

Z

Oksun Kang 강옥선

부산대학교에서 박사학위 취득, 동서대학교 영어학과 교수

저서

『19세기 영국여성의 글쓰기』(동인, 2013)
Elements of English Poetry (신아사, 2011), 공저
『블레이크와 작은 천국』(동인, 2004), 공저

논문

「블레이크의 예언시에서 불의 이미지 읽기」(2009)

Steven Reeder 스티븐 리더

캘리포니아 주립대학 석사학위 취득, 경성대학교 영어영문학과 교수

저서

Illuminated Short Stories in English (신아사, 2017), 공저
An Introduction to English and American Literature (신아사, 2015), 공저
Exploring English Short Stories (신아사, 2010), 공저
Eternal Spirit of the Chainless Mind (신아사, 2007), 공저

논문

"Reclaiming Eden: Conquering Thanatophobia in Aronofsky's *The Fountain*" (2011)
"Dracula as a Tragic Hero: The Illumination of Film on a Text" (2006)

Hyosun An 안효선(삽화 디자이너)

Academy of Art University, Fine Arts 석사학위 취득
이화여자대학교 박사학위 취득, 이화여대 의류산업학과 전임연구원

저서

Illuminated Short Stories in English (신아사, 2017), 삽화

논문

디자인분야에서 빅데이터를 활용한 감성평가 방법 모색(2016)
"A Conceptual Framework for Asian Women's Emotional Needs in Fashion Design" (2015)
수상 대한민국 신미술대전 제 32회 패션 일러스트레이션 부문 대상

POETICS: An Illustrated Guide
초판 1쇄 발행 _ 2018년 11월 30일

공　　저 • 강 옥 선 · 스티븐 리더
발 행 인 • 정 현 걸
발　　행 • 신 아 사
인　　쇄 • 대명프린팅
출판등록 • 1956년 1월 5일 (제9-52호)
주　　소 • 서울시 은평구 통일로 59길 4(2층)
전　　화 • 02)382-6411 · 팩스 02)382-6401
홈페이지 • www.shinasa.co.kr
E-MAIL • shinasa@daum.net

ISBN 978-89-8396-297-3 (93840)

정가 15,000 원